THE
SONGWRITER'S
HANDBOOK

THE
SONGWRITER'S
HANDBOOK

Tom T. Hall

RUTLEDGE HILL PRESS
Nashville, Tennessee 37210

Published by Rutledge Hill Press, a Thomas Nelson Company, P. O. Box 141000, Nashville, Tennessee 37214.

Previous edition published as *How I Write Songs, Why You Can* by Chappell Music, Nashville, Tennessee.

Typography by ProtoType Graphics, Inc., Nashville, Tennessee.

Library of Congress Cataloging-in-Publication Data

Hall, Tom T.
    The songwriter's handbook
    ISBN 1-55853-860-7
    Rev ed. of: How I write songs, why you can, © 1976.
    Discography : p.
    Includes Index.
    1. Music, Popular (Songs, etc.)—Writing and publishing.
I. Hall, Tom T. How I write songs, why you can. II. Title.
III. Title: Songwriters handbook.
MT67.H25   1987
784.5'028   87-9468
                                                        CIP

Printed in the United States of America

To Dee Evans, who said,
"Haven't I Been Good to You?"

And if there come the singers and the dancers and the flute players, —buy of their gifts also.

For they too are gatherers of fruit and frankincense, and that which they bring, though fashioned of dreams, is raiment and food for the soul.

Kahlil Gibran, *The Prophet*

Contents

"Ravishing Ruby"
"Don't Forget the Coffee, Billy Joe"
How I Wrote "I Love"
More Song Lyrics

Preface

There was a time when I thought songs came out of a factory. I assumed that somewhere, in some giant, providence-oriented building, there were thousands and maybe millions of records with songs on them, and that every now and then they took a few out of storage and sent them around to record shops and radio stations. I was six or seven years old at the time, so the notion did not seem far fetched. It was with this notion in mind that I sought to play a trick on my friends; I would write a song. When, at the age of nine, I had accomplished this feat, I was surprised that other people in my neighborhood had also written songs and that this was where they came from; people wrote them.

How utterly amazed I was to find myself in the select company of such writers as Hank Williams, Ernest Tubb, Fred Rose, and Irving Berlin, broadly speaking. It was a wonderful feeling, and so I continued to write songs, even though I had no idea that people would someday pay me to do so.

I was at a neighbor's house. They were newlyweds, and they were having their first fight. I was their witness. The woman screamed at her husband, "I'm going home to Mother!"

The husband replied in a sad voice, "Haven't I been good to you?"

I remember saying to myself, "Now there's a good idea to write a song about."

That was my first song.

Introduction

The music business has its own language by which its people communicate. Like other areas of society, words and expressions often mean something different in the music business than they do in the world at large. To help you read this book, and to help you in dealing with the business, I have included two lists of words and expressions commonly used.

Some Definitions of Terms Used in the Music Business

Song: A musical entity, complete in itself, that expresses to the listener whatever the writer is trying to convey.

Verse: A segment of a song; a division of thought development within the song. Verses usually repeat themselves melodically.

Bridge: A song segment with a melodic progression different from the verses. It is used to break up repetition in the tune and for building momentum and dramatic value. The terms *chorus* and *refrain* are also used for this segment, especially when the same lyrics are used each time the bridge is inserted.

Modulation: The changing of the key or pitch of a song within a particular performance of it.

Copyright: A legal statement of song ownership, registered with the Library of Congress.

Record (REH-cord): Phonograph recording of a song, usually identified more with the singer than with the writer of the song.

Record (reh-KORD): The electronic-mechanical process of preserving sound for later listening; *cut* is a similar term.

Recording Studio: A facility specifically designed and equipped for recording.

Recording Session: The specific time (in a studio) when music is recorded. *Master session* means music is intended to be released for sale to the public; *demo session* means songs are being recorded strictly to demonstrate to recording artists and record companies the potential of material. *Work tape* refers to the simple recording of a song in the early stage of idea development when it probably needs further revision; *spec session* (similar to a *custom session*) applies to a recording made with hopes of interesting a company in releasing the finished product.

Mastering: The process of transferring sound from tape (produced in the studio) to a disc *(acetate).*

Pressing Plant: A facility specifically designed for manufacturing phonograph records from the mastered disc.

Recording Company (often referred to as the *label*): A firm that sells recorded music; it may or may not have its own studio, as studio facilities are available on a rental basis.

Publishing Company: In music, a firm making song material available to recording companies; in effect, the step between the songwriter and the recording artist. *Publishing house* applies mostly to book publishers.

Performance Rights, Societies: The organizations that collect fees permitting the use of licensed music, then disburse the money to writers.

Distributor: The firm engaged in wholesaling records.

Producer: A representative of a recording company; the one responsible for coordinating all the aspects of a recording session, such as song material, musicianship, and technical details.

Engineer: The person who operates the recording equipment.

Promo Man: A person employed to attract the attention of DJs and salespeople to the product of a certain recording company or publishing company.

Songwriter: A person who writes songs, presumably for a living. In the public's eye (especially in newspapers) this includes anyone who says he is a songwriter, regardless of whether he has written any songs or had them recorded.

Hot writer: Someone getting a lot of songs cut.

Cold writer: Someone not getting a lot of songs cut.

Artist: In the music business, this usually refers to a featured singer or performer; a "star."

Picker: In the Nashville vernacular, any musician, regardless of the instrument or type of music.

Union Musician: A member of the American Federation of Musicians, who will work for no less than a set rate or "scale" for a particular type of work.

Scab session: The use of nonunion musicians, who are paid less than scale.

Hobby picker (hobby writer): Someone involved in the music business as a sideline. Some of these people make substantial contributions to the industry and have good reasons for not getting into it exclusively.

Spook (bug): A person who continuously, without any regard for privacy, schedules, or other commitments, keeps bothering someone in the music business with songs, ideas, or adoration.

Squirrelly: Used to explain otherwise unexplainable behavior of someone in the music business.

Hit: A successful song (there may be several records of the same song, any of which may or may not be hits themselves).

Smash: A super hit.

Smasheroo: A super smash (*monster* is a similar term).

Bomb: A song (or record) that proved unsuccessful (*dog, dud, piece of crap* are similar terms that frequently apply to material considered unfit to record).

Hype: Unfounded praise; bullshit.

Some Music Business Expressions and What They Mean

"We cut some stuff yesterday that'll scare you." He recorded some
music he thinks you'll like.

*"That blew my hat in the creek," "It wore me out," "It knocked me down,"
". . . warped my mind."* He liked it.

"Wow! That's heavy!" He likes it, probably because of some profound
statement or implication in the song material.

"I don't know; that's a little heavy." He thinks that piece of material
may be too profound for public understanding and acceptance.

"I got four songs placed today." Four songs were accepted for recording (may refer to publishing among writers not affiliated
with a certain publishing company).

"I got two songs cut last week." These songs were actually recorded.
Sometimes material "accepted" never gets to the studio; so
it's more important to have it actually cut.

"My Jerry Lee record is set for release Tuesday." The finished version
of a song recorded by Jerry Lee Lewis will be placed on sale
at that time.

*"We just used two guitars and a bass on that session today, but it's cut
on sixteen tracks, so we can overdub the Nashville Symphony if
we want to."* In recording on multiple-track tape (usually 2, 4,
8, or 16) it is common practice to put part of the musical
accompaniment on tape at a time. *Overdubbing* is the adding
of a new sound to previously recorded sound. *The Nashville
Symphony* often refers to a large number of string players
on a session who may or may not be members of the symphony.

"We're mixing today." The producer, engineer, and maybe the recording artist will go into the studio to get a final balance of
the various tracks on the recording. No musicians need be
present unless some overdubbing is needed.

"Gotta new song? Well, lay it on me." Let me hear it.

"I've had two single covers and six album cuts on my Jerry Lee record."
Two single recordings by different artists have been made

since the original recording, and the song has been included in six different albums.

THE SONGWRITER'S HANDBOOK

CHAPTER 1

What Is a Song?

I bet you thought you could answer that question before you bought this book. However, what you hear on your radio or your record player is not really a song. What you hear is an arrangement, a vocal styling, a production, harmony, mixing, editing, overdubbing, mastering, and on and on into who knows where.

There are all kinds of musical compositions in the world: classical music, music to complement the dance, interludes of all sorts, background music for movies and TV—you know the rest. This book is about songwriting and has little or nothing to do with any of the above.

So when composing a song, please try to forget about what you hear on your radio. All the rest comes later.

A song is a poem set to music. When the words are set to music by the lonely composer there is one melody line, written with the accompaniment of a single instrument such as a piano or guitar. It is not possible to compose a song-poem with a twenty-eight piece orchestra. An orchestra might be invited to play it after it has been arranged, but the songwriter must start alone with the simple, single melody and an instrument.

Now I think we can sit down and consider a song.

Let's take "Jingle Bells." We are not permitted to print the song here but you're probably familiar with it. This is a song where the person or persons who wrote it knew what they were talking about. They speak of bells on bobtails; they mention a one horse open sleigh and tell you where to ride it (through the fields); they explain the kind of surface on which to ride it (snow); and they make it sound like fun. Get the idea? It's a *good* song. We want to write songs like that, good ones, wherein we know what we are talking about. And doesn't "Jingle Bells" have a catchy melody? Not complicated, but catchy.

For the most part, songs usually tell a story. They are good poems that are written in meter and rhyme. "Irene, Goodnight" is a fine example of a song that tells a story, and almost everyone has heard it at one time or another. Remember the story? The person gets married; he and his wife part; and at the end he's thinking of jumping into the river. It doesn't sound like much of a plot, but it's a great song.

In this book I hope to tell you a great deal about how song-writers work and live. There are chapters on almost, if not every, problem that a songwriter might encounter. If you are able to imagine what the man who invented the can opener would have done with it if he had invented it before the can was invented, you can get an idea of what problems you'll face if you write a song and don't know what to do with it.

I was teaching a course in songwriting at Middle Tennessee State University when a student came to me and said, "This is all wonderful information and I've learned a lot, but you didn't tell us how to write a hit song."

I have news for him, and you. Between you, the songwriter, and the record shop or radio, there are hundreds of people who will have a hand in the finished product. Nobody knows a hit song before it's a hit. And these hundreds of people all have a hand in the make-or-break stages of production. Try not to be concerned with whether or not your song will be a hit. Get it down the best you can, and let the people who are in charge of production worry about their jobs.

Above all else, have some fun. That's what songs are all about.

On a scholarly note, a song is a primitive, monophonic, poetical composition. If you can't unravel that, don't worry. That's what this book is supposed to do for you.

CHAPTER 2

Are Songwriters Born?

I once read an article about Albert Einstein. It said that as a very young man he was not interested in or very adept at mathematics. It was only when a member of his family interested him in algebra—they were playing games at finding "Mr. X"—that Einstein really became interested in mathematics. And you know the rest of his story.

Are some people born songwriters? I think so. Some people have the ability to pick up a guitar or sit down at a piano and immediately begin composing great melodies and writing great lyrics. But I think that somewhere, at some time, even born writers were inspired to pursue their talents, to cultivate them, and to broaden their knowledge of the gift for which they had an instinct and inclination. They became better writers than they would have been if they hadn't worked at it.

If you are a born writer, a lot of the information I have here is not going to be important to you. It will be sort of second nature to you. What I tell you will be more or less like my trying to teach a fish to swim.

However, I maintain that anyone who wants to be a writer—and a songwriter in particular—must work at it, because songwriting is as much a craft as it is a talent. In order to write songs, you have to be able to recognize what a song is. You have to be able to recognize the importance of something that is entertaining, and you have to say what you want to say very briefly.

I believe there are many great natural-born songwriters and that there are craftsmen, too, and I know people in Nashville who have made money in both instances. I know of a time when a man

Tom T. whittles and thinks.

was recording an album of truck songs in Nashville, and they needed another cut. Within the hour, one of Nashville's popular songwriters had written a song and had gotten it to the session, and they recorded it. That song was not written because the song-writer was inspired or because it had been written earlier and was just waiting around for the right moment. It happened because a professional, a craftsman, a man who had worked hard in the industry, was called on to do a job and did it. The song was needed for the album, and it made money.

Some people have become songwriters not because they had any natural gift for it, but because of their tremendous drive and interest in songwriting. I know very successful songwriters in

Nashville today who at one time could hardly write their own names. Now I know that's an old cliché we use for people who can't write, but there really are people in Nashville who have loved songwriting, who have studied it and worked at it, and who have become proficient and professional at it even though they didn't seem to be born songwriters. This is not to say these people are hacks, a term we use for someone who pounds out a set of words or someone who just concocts a melody from two or three different melodies and goes on about his business. These people have worked at perfecting their craft until their creativity shows through. Even though they were writing things that seemed unimportant at one time, now they are writing interesting songs. While they were finding themselves and discovering what they would like to write, they were polishing their craft. I think this is very important. The two processes go together very well.

In some instances a fellow has great ideas for some songs, but he just doesn't know how to write them. Then there are instances where a fellow knows a great deal about how to write songs, but he doesn't seem to have the inspiration; he just isn't in contact with what people consider entertaining. The ability to write a song can eventually mesh with the inspiration necessary to get it on its way to being born. All people reach a point in life when they have some creative thoughts they would like to communicate. And if over the years the craft of songwriting has been polished, then ideas will get together with technique and songs will see the light of day.

Even if you are a born songwriter, if you do not polish your craft and learn all the ins and outs of the music and the songwriting businesses, I believe you will have wasted a good deal of your talent. You won't have the mechanics to go with the creativity.

Take advantage of everything there is to learn from the great albums and music. Study them. Even though you may never become a professional songwriter, I guarantee that you will have one of the greatest hobbies in the world. I know, because I was a hobbyist for many years before I became a professional.

CHAPTER 3

Rules and Tools

favorite expression among songwriters—especially those of us who have had our share of successes and disappoint-ments—is "there are no rules in songwriting." I think this maxim appeared because at one time or another all of us have been confused and startled by a completely unorthodox song that be-came a tremendous hit. It didn't follow the formula, or pattern, of what we consider a standard song. I think that's why we tend to pass off the oddities and left-field hits by saying there are no rules in songwriting.

Unfortunately, however, the saying is not true. Like every other profession, songwriting does have its rules; and while you don't have to adhere to them, you have to know what they are before you break them. That's why I'm giving them to you here.

A Line Should Stand Alone

One good rule to remember—and, I repeat, it's not important that you adhere to these rules all the time—is that a line should stand alone. A line in a song should be a complete thought, even though it must rhyme with the following line or the line thereafter. It should be a sentence.

Here is an example:

The water was very cold.

Now that line stands alone. It says something. It has all the parts a sentence has to have.

The next line, which should also stand alone, is (and here we are writing a little song):

The traveler was very bold.

Now you have two lines that stand alone:

The water was very cold.
The traveler was very bold.

While they have continuity in themselves, they're telling you about the water being very cold. We could substitute *swimmer* for *traveler,* and maybe we should.

The water was very cold.
The swimmer was very bold.

These two lines stand alone. Each is a complete thought.
Here is an example of two lines that do not stand alone:

The water in the well
Was cold as hell

These two lines don't stand alone. *The water in the well* doesn't do anything; it doesn't go anywhere. And *was cold as hell* doesn't say anything completely. So you have two lines that say the water in the well was cold as hell. It rhymes and eventually says something, but each line does not stand alone; you need the second line to make sense out of the first. That violates one of the rules that most songwriters believe in and subscribe to: When you have a line, make that line say something and then go on to the next line and say something with it.

Although we can't repeat its lyrics here, a song by the very good songwriter Liz Anderson—Lynn Anderson's mother—is a classic example of lines standing alone: "From Now On All of My Friends Are Gonna Be Strangers." Each line in the song made a definite statement, and each statement made a point. I would recommend it as an example. If you adhere to this rule as much as possible, your songs will have much more clarity. They'll be better understood and better accepted.

Avoid Connecting Words If You Can

When it comes to having a line stand alone, it is very important to do away with *but*, *so*, and *and*. Let's go back to our first sample line:

The water was very cold.

Let's make the second line:

But the swimmer was very bold.

Although some people have a tendency to tie the lines together with connecting words, I recommend—and have heard it recommended by other writers—that you do away with such connectives. A lot of people use them when they are not needed. I don't know why people have a tendency to do this. I've had songs where the singer who recorded them added a lot of and's and but's when there was no need because I had tried to make the lines in my songs stand alone. Let's just do away with them as useless unless you absolutely need one to clarify a point.

Keep It Short

I learned one of my greatest lessons in the army. One of my officers told me to write a letter to base headquarters and tell them that our runway was too short to land the type of plane they were bringing into our area. Like most young writers, I sat down to make a big impression on my superiors. So this letter:

Dear Sirs:
It has come to our attention that you will be arriving at our base on 16 April in an air personnel transport. It is our displeasure to inform you that the area to which we have access is not . . .

Then I began another letter:

Dear Sirs:
Due to the area provided us by the area air personnel director as provided for in AM 273–609 we are . . .

Then I wrote the letter I should have written in the first place:

Dear Sirs:
Our runway is too short.

Getting right to the point can save you a lot of time and trouble. I admit that making a complex idea sound simple is not the easiest thing in the world to do. Sometimes we endanger our ability to communicate by the way we go about trying to do it. I am sure you have heard many a movie general tell a flustered private to "Get on with it, man!" You really do need to get on with it. The space you have in a song is not much. If you are going to beat around the bush for three minutes, you will find your time is up, your song is gone, and you are left with a good song in your mouth. Just say it!

I like the story about Abe Lincoln's once saying he could make an hour-long speech right now, but it would take him all day to write a three-minute speech. That's why songwriters have to study their craft; when you have only a few dozen words to make your point and two or three minutes to do it in, you have to get to it right away.

Think Positive

Keep your thoughts happy, and always have a hero in your song. If you are going to be nagging or critical, or put someone down, have the singer or the main character in the song on the winning side.

It's unusual for a song that puts something down in a nagging sort of negative way to be successful. The positive thought is the best thought, although my "Harper Valley P.T.A.," where the young lady put down the entire P.T.A., might seem to be an exception.

Disparaging the P.T.A. in that song made a moral point, and it was directed against a particular class of people, not against individuals. Had I written a song where Jeannie C. Riley was putting down Shirley Thompson for her drinking, I don't think it would have been a success. It would have been just a song about what a terrible person Shirley Thompson was for drinking before she came to the P.T.A. meeting. But it is a sort of protest song against the classes. And it is a song with the old successful plot where someone fights city hall and wins.

So, when I talk about not writing negative songs, I don't mean that you should never write anything negative about anyone. But I am saying that you should keep your thoughts positive.

The Title Is the Point

Another rule, one I have broken probably more times than anybody else in country music songwriting, is: Repeat the title of the song often. Make your point. You don't *have* to stick to this rule; not everybody does, and I seldom do. Sometimes my songs don't have the titles in them anywhere. For instance, "Homecoming," a favorite of mine, doesn't have the word *homecoming* in it at all. Another favorite, and one of my most successful records, was "The Ballad of Forty Dollars," and not once in the song did I say "ballad of forty dollars."

Yet, you ought to keep this rule in mind. Make sure that throughout the song you make reference to what you're singing about, which, of course, is the title of the song. A lot of people follow this rule with great success. Because of the nature of my songs, I don't always follow it myself, I still recommend it to you. Don't write a song that needs the title repeated often and then leave it out. Always make sure you have your audience in mind when writing your song so you can tell them what your song's about.

Avoid Too Much Realism

Other rules, I suppose, should be called peculiarities. For example, it may not be to the commercial advantage of your song to use a name that is unusual, like Agatha, Allistair, or Egbert unless that name consistently conjures up a certain picture. Names have a way of doing that. Your characters probably should have rather common-sounding names, and you should change the names from the actual story that prompted you to write.

That's a good idea: Avoid being too realistic, tying your songs too closely to real people. Otherwise you'll end up making someone angry with you because it was easy to identify him. Especially in the case of story songs, like the kind I write, it can be virtually impossible to keep peace with everybody.

I got a telegram just before a concert one night telling me that if I performed a certain song that evening I could expect a lawsuit. "The song is about my brother, and it is not true," said the wire. Well, if the story was not true about that lady's brother, it must not have been about her brother, wouldn't you suppose? Somebody's brother, perhaps, but not hers.

Although many of my songs come from real life situations, in the treatment of the story I make no effort to stifle my freedom as a creative artist. The skies around those cypress trees that Vincent Van Gogh painted weren't really swirls of blues and purples; but that's how he saw them, and that's how he wanted you to be able to see them. The same principle applies to my songs.

Use Good Taste

If you have a line for a song that makes reference to something very personal or embarrassing to you or someone else, throw it out. Use good taste. To show you what I mean, let me tell you a story about an incident that happened to me.

I was in a music store buying a set of guitar strings when a young fellow came in and said, "You're Tom T. Hall," and I said, "Yes, sir, I am." He said, "I'm glad I ran into you today because I have something here you wouldn't believe." He ran to the rack of guitars on the wall, grabbed one down, and started tuning it. I thought it was a rather inappropriate time to sing me a song, but he came back to the counter where I was standing, took me by the arm, and said, "My mother died about a week ago and I wrote the damnedest song about it you've ever heard." Now, I think he should have drawn a line before he went that far.

You have to use good judgment in what you write about. You can't say just anything in a song. While it's important to be realistic and individualistic, let's not roar off into some private matter that's going to embarrass you, your friends, your neighbors, your family and everybody else. You have to draw a line somewhere, even if it's only in your mind.

Whatever is acceptable in everyday conversation ought to be suitable enough to put into a song. If you want to write about those things that are not polite conversation, let's clothe them in respectable language, as you would if you were discussing some sensitive subject in public.

Don't Have a Singer on Your Mind

When Francis Scott Key wrote "The Star-Spangled Banner" on that morning when the war was raging and the flag was flying and the bombs were bursting in the air—which, incidentally, gives you some indication of the types of people who write songs—would you imagine that he had someone in mind to sing that song? I seriously doubt it.

On many occasions you will hear writers say, "This song is just right for ol' so-and-so." If you have a song you think is just right for Michael Jackson or Alabama or Frank Sinatra, in all honesty you're kidding yourself.

I'll tell you why this is so. A songwriter must be very careful not to count his chickens before they hatch. I know that's another old cliché, but let me say that if you keep hearing Frank Sinatra singing it while you're writing, the song will take on much more respectability than it deserves. In your mind you already have it recorded, even before you have it written! And, unfortunately, that hinders your objectivity about the material.

When you're writing a song, don't worry about whether it's going to make any money. Don't worry about whether someone is going to record it, and don't try to think of any particular person singing it. All those distractions have a way of leading you complacently into the wrong lyrics and a contrived melody.

If I'm writing a song and hear Frank Sinatra singing it as I go along, I think, "Well, I have heard a lot of people say that Frank Sinatra can sing anything." If you do this you may be writing a song with no merit or meaning—no message, no reason, and no rhyme—but you're hearing Frank Sinatra sing and it sounds great!

Maybe it's trash, but you hear the Rolling Stones banging it out on the stage at a rock concert while thousands of people cheer.

Songs should not be listened to in that mental context. To begin with, when you concentrate on the trappings you lose the lyrics and melodies; the fantasies become the important thing to you, not what you're writing. When you're dreaming of the fanfare with the lights flashing and you up in the spotlight getting your reward for writing the greatest song of the century before you even get it down on paper—then you're kidding yourself.

So let's try not to do the bit about "this song is just right for so-and-so."

Keep Current

One word of caution: "Keeping current" and "copy-catting" are two different things. In the earliest stages of your songwriting, it's not a bad idea to do a little imitating of songs that impress you. Reworking and reshuffling the songs of others can help you learn the subtleties of song construction. But as your craft emerges as an outlet for your ideas, try to express these thoughts through your own individuality. Don't try to flood the market with rewrites of songs that are already popular.

It's difficult to avoid being influenced by the songs of others. We are influenced, and that's what "keeping current" means. But don't expect to get a lot of your songs published and recorded if all you have on your demo tape is a collection of watered-down versions of currently popular songs. It's not a disgrace to be one of the sheep, but there's considerably more glory (and money) in being a shepherd.

CHAPTER 4

Hang-ups

O ne of the biggest problems a writer has is getting rid of hang-ups, complexes he may develop about his geography, background, education, family, race, creed, or color. Geography is one of the big hang-ups a writer can sometimes have, such as being born in New York City and wanting to write a country song, or being born in Dothan, Alabama, and wanting to write a serious Broadway musical. Being from New York City will not help you in writing a Broadway musical, nor will being from Dothan, Alabama, help you write a country song.

Cities and Countries

Songs are an international pastime. Many successful ones have been written about places and people the writers knew nothing about. For example, I understand that "South of the Border" was written by two gentlemen from Great Britain who had never been south of the border down Mexico way. So whether you are from the country or the city, write any sort of song you please, any kind of music you like.

For many years the country boy had a hang-up about being from the country. He knew many city folk associated the word *country* with illiteracy, ignorance, poverty, and backwardness.

However, if you stop to think about it, until the 1930s life in the United States was predominantly of a rural nature. There were big cities, of course, but the great migration to them had not yet occurred. So at the time many of us were born, the majority of the people in the United States were country people. They lived away from the cities, and it was necessary for them to have cows and chickens and know something about farm life. Even if they didn't actively participate in farming, they were well aware of it.

Being from the country is just a matter of where you were born. It doesn't have anything to do with your ability to write or not to write, to succeed or not to succeed. By the same token, being from the city does not mean you can't write songs about cowboys and Indians, coal miners, people from Appalachia, or anything else you choose to write about. So geography would be one hang-up I would like you to rid yourself of; songwriting is free of all boundaries.

Honest Feelings

If you intend to write songs that are popular only among people like you, you will be limiting your success as a songwriter. We must write for the nation as a whole and for the world. When you write your songs, don't be concerned about where you're from.

More importantly, be concerned that your song honestly reflects your feelings about a particular subject. Someone once said that when you write about yourself, you write about the universe, for we are all much alike in our basic emotions.

Fact and Fantasy

If people take you so seriously that they think you would never lean toward fiction in your songwriting, then writing songs about your sweetheart—whether wife or girlfriend—would be a very perilous bit of creative activity. However, if people know you have a creative streak, those who are in close contact with your writing and ideas and the kind of music you like will readily understand that songwriting is a creative process. You may be writing about the past, or you may be writing about the present. You may be writing about your own love problems or those of someone with whom you are acquainted. So don't pass up the idea for a great song because you think it might embarrass your wife or your girlfriend, or someone else near you.

Pablo Picasso defined art as "a lie that tells the truth." Sometimes we can indeed get closer to the truth of a subject by creating an imaginary situation based on it, rather than by giving a blow-by-blow account. We seldom have the opportunity to know all the facts, and any account is likely to lack at least some of "truth." But if we create our own story, the elements of it are all true (if they are believable) because we made them so.

To write a hit song, you have to say something. Sometimes it may offend a few of your friends, or maybe even your husband or wife. You may step on a few toes, but I think you'd do well not to succumb to the hang-ups you will no doubt encounter as you pursue your songwriting career. If you find something worth writing about, then write it. Say what you will, and then, if you're not absolutely sure you want to show it to anyone, lay it aside. Have a safe place where you can lock up your writing when you have finished; a small box with a little lock on it will do. Just tell the inquisitive that these things are private notes, much like a diary.

As for writer hang-ups, don't worry about geography, don't worry about creed. Don't worry about color or religion. Think of yourself as entertaining the world, not just your immediate surroundings. Try to see a broader use of your songs than what you will immediately find.

Excuses, Excuses

There are more excuses for not writing than there are for not going on a diet or not going for a thorough physical check-up. With so many reasons for putting off writing that big hit, it's a wonder most records have any music on them. Let's kill a few of these little demons that keep you from being rich and famous.

"I've had a lot on my mind." Quite the contrary. If you had a lot on your mind, you'd have something to write about.

"I've got to have peace and quiet." Bullshit! Francis Scott Key wrote "The Star-Spangled Banner" in the middle of a battle.

"Why write? No one listens to my songs." No one listens to your stomach yet you eat, don't you?

"The music business is all a big clique; they don't want any new writers." The Miami Dolphins are a big clique; try out for the team.

"I'm afraid someone would steal my songs." It would be the greatest compliment you could get.

"I don't have a guitar." Buy one.

"I don't have a typewriter." Buy one.

"I don't have any melodies." Borrow one.

CHAPTER 5

The Time, the Place, the Attitude

When I first started writing songs professionally, I was working at a radio station in West Virginia. As the program director, I wrote most of the copy or commercials that went on the air. I had a small office that I became very fond of after a year or so because it was rather ragtag. It had a lot of my things on the wall, pictures and notes and scraps of paper. There were numerous cigarette burns around the edge of the old desk caused by my dashing off suddenly to the control room to tell someone that we weren't selling a certain item at a certain price, or to correct some other goof that I had miswritten into the copy. It was a very comfortable place.

In those days I did a lot of writing. I took information from newspaper ads and put it into some logical order for radio listeners, since we were trying to sell some of the merchandise that the stores had. After about a year of writing radio copy, I began writing songs, too. My first two or three songs were for NewKeys Music. The first one I ever had recorded was "D. J. for a Day," and another was "Artificial Rose," recorded by Jimmy C. Newman. For Dave Dudley I wrote "Mad," which was a BMI award winner. I was going great.

One day I went to Nashville to talk to my publisher and to have a little vacation. When I returned, the enterprising people with whom I worked had redecorated my office. They had taken all the little notes off the walls, repaired the desk, removed the cigarette burns, cleaned the beer cans and empty whiskey bottles out of the closet, painted the place, and put in a new rug.

The new decor was nice—perhaps—but it disturbed the mood

for writing I had developed in that room. It must have taken me three or four months before I finally got to where I could write there again.

Find (or Make) a Place

You may find that your place to write is your kitchen, the bedroom, the garage, on top of the house, the attic, the bathroom. But wherever, you will need a definite place. All the rejected tapes will be stashed there, songs you have played for people but they rejected. Maybe you'll have copies of your records on the wall; many people have them made into plaques. You'll have little notes from other writers and pictures of yourself.

All of these things help you settle your mind and get comfortable with writing; they make your attitude toward writing more professional. If you have all your accouterments stashed in a carton in an attic, then your writing is not brought to mind as often as it should be. But if you have a small spot you can call your writing place, it will be a great advantage to you.

Over the years I have had small offices in which I could write well for some reason or another, like the one in West Virginia. In one house that I lived in I had a bedroom that seemed to lend itself well to writing songs. Now I have a paneled and carpeted room in my barn. I also have there a collection of research and reference books, such as my thesaurus and my rhyming dictionary and a copy of *The Wit and Humor of Mark Twain*, which I occasionally like to refer to. If I become bored with my writing, I'll read a little Mark Twain.

You should have a favorite writer whom you like to read when you want to refresh your mind and get away from an idea temporarily. If you can come back to it later, the idea will probably flow stronger.

A place where you can write is very important. I would suggest that you find one and stick with it. At first it may seem a little uncomfortable, a little too put-together; but keep doodling with the innovations that give it your individuality. My barn seemed a little mechanical at first, but now I have written a couple of albums there and I feel very warm and comfortable in it.

Equipment You'll Need

You probably will need a tape recorder. It will let you hear how your song sounds, no matter how well you sing. The standard equipment is a cassette recorder, the kind you find in classrooms.

A typewriter is extremely helpful, although it is not essential. If you happen to own or have access to a carbon-ribbon, vari-type electric typewriter, fine—but a portable will do just as well, provided the finished typed page is legible. That's the purpose of using a typewriter in the first place—not to make a fancy impression, but to make the lyrics of your song legible. If you cannot get to a typewriter, be careful to make your handwriting clear and easy to read. The people who will be reviewing your song material do not have time to struggle to make out a word. Besides, it is impolite to put them in a position of having to struggle to decipher a scrawl.

The guitar or piano you use for your recording, like the recorder and typewriter, doesn't have to be fancy, but it should be adequate. It's as difficult to listen to a recording of an out-of-tune, raspy, rattling guitar or piano as it is to try to read a hen-scratch lyric. Don't create any problems for yourself by making your material difficult or unpleasant to review.

Finding Time to Write

You need more than just a place in which you can write; you need the time, too. This is very important.

I am writing these words at a small desk in a room of my house where I do some of my writing. It is 5:30 A.M. I do most of my writing in the early morning hours, after I've had a good night's sleep. When I'm refreshed and have had some coffee, and perhaps a cigarette, and everyone else in the house is asleep, it is a very good time for me to write.

I know a lot of people write best in the afternoon, while others prefer the morning or late in the evening. Many writers tell me they write between three and five o'clock in the morning after they have been up all night. I do a lot of writing at that time of day too, but normally I get a good night's sleep first. When I'm up early and my mind is fresh and clear, I have a renewed interest in what's

Basic songwriting equipment you'll need.

going on in the world and feel that I have an advantage over other people. I am sure there are very few people up then writing songs about war and peace, and love and hate.

I recommend that you try writing at different times of the day to find which suits you best. Then you can know when you are most creative, when you have your best thoughts and make good decisions.

It is very important to get yourself on a schedule. Even though you may not write anything during that half hour or hour you have set aside for writing, at least you will know you have dedicated a part of your time and effort to becoming a songwriter.

You should discipline yourself to spend some time each day writing or reviewing something you have written, or perhaps studying or listening to someone else's music. Devote an hour or two, depending on your interest.

When to Write . . . and When Not to Write

Writers will sometimes wait for weeks until an opening line comes to them. I have kept a song idea around for months waiting for the right approach to the lyrics and the melody. When the day comes that your song starts to move for you, the most obvious opening line will start it. Sometimes we writers oversimplify a dramatic idea or overstate a simple one. Be as honest as you can as you write, and you will find the opening lines coming more easily.

The story is told of a songwriter who was on a plane for New York and when the plane stopped in Atlanta turned to his manager and said, "Get me off this damned plane and to a piano, quick! I have a great idea for a song!"

That was the right time for him to write. The iron was hot, and he struck. When you have an idea for a song and it's ready in your mind, get it down somewhere on something, somehow.

But just as there's a time to write, there's also a time to wait. That's when you don't know exactly what you want to say. When I have ideas for songs but no titles or melodies and no earthly idea what the lyrics will turn out to be, I call them "germs." On the other hand, sometimes I have a notion that is so broad and so deep that I know the thought I want to convey, but I am unsure of the vehicle with which I would like to transport it.

Let's pretend that you have had what you consider a great notion about a summer morning. There are many things that can be done on a summer morning. An idea like this—a feeling or an attitude—can become a great song, but the idea has to develop in your mind. You have to let the idea take shape and bloom.

It is not always possible to get right to the point of a concept. When you can't come to an immediate conclusion about what you want to say or the mood you want to set—wait. If it is a good idea, it will grow and your song will come. It is when you know full well what you have in mind that you want to go ahead and write. Get it down on tape or paper. Spit it out. Rock on!

Try not to let the obvious "nose-on-your-face" ideas buffalo you, and don't let the subtle little "germs" mystify you. Jump on one and wait on the other. You can afford to wait for an idea to grow. You

At work.

are going to be writing songs for a long time. You'll catch that little "germ" rascal, and when you have him caged you will have captured a part of all that there is.

Rainy Days for Writers

Some days when you are sitting with your guitar or at your piano, life can feel pretty grim. Words won't come, your melodies are all like something else you've heard, and music rattles through your brain like a train over an old bridge. If you are a real writer, these things will not discourage you. In fact, the trials of a writer in distress often benefit those who find a real wingding of a song rolling off the mental presses at a later time.

Only by knowing how difficult it can be at times can a writer experience the joy of having a song born in the air around his head. I have seen writers roll out of their self-imposed exile of a week or two with a smile as wide as a watermelon slice, yelling, "I've written a song that weighs ten pounds!"

"What's it about?"

"It's about this old boy and this old girl."

Then you smile and say to yourself, "Ah, yes. The good ones always are."

Rainy days for writers are the ones when no one wants to listen to your songs. They also are the days when you don't want to listen to your songs either. On days when you don't like your own songs, by examining your thoughts, you will find you don't like other people's songs either. Some days music doesn't do anything for you; you'll have to get used to having those days.

I heard the story of a man who had taken his talents to be reviewed in New York City. He said, "On those cold days when you think you have nothing to say, when you feel you have no talent, your heart will cry out in anguish to know if anyone cares. If the answer is 'Hell, no!' you know you're in New York City." We all have our little trips to New York, but we also have our days when our new songs weigh ten pounds.

I have sat for hours looking at a typewriter or a pencil and strumming my guitar with an absolute absence of inspiration. I'll be leaning back in my chair, chewing on a pencil, wondering how they built the pyramids, wondering how the president of the United States of America feels when he gets constipated, and wondering if Shakespeare ever got constipated and hoping he did.

The big question then is, "Will I ever write a song? Or will I ever write another song?" On rainy days you know you never will. When the sun comes out, you know it was foolish to believe that.

I overheard this routine between a songwriter and a disc jockey.

"Do you ever get the feeling you'll never write another hit?"

"Every damned day."

"Don't be discouraged" is trite advice to a person who "will never write another hit." But I know writers who have said time and again that they had "cooled off" and who were writing almost everything important in music a year later.

Music is a fad-oriented form of entertainment. What's hot in music today may be old hat tomorrow. The things you are writing right now may be big next year.

One of my favorite writers, Harlan Howard, once told me, "I never throw away anything I've written." I think that's good advice.

If you can't use a line in the song you are working on now, you may come back to it another day and find it's exactly what you need.

Save those bits and pieces
of your mind.
The thinking you are doing now
may be a different kind.
The nut or bolt you throw away
because it doesn't fit
May someday save the sinking
of the ship.

T.T.H.

CHAPTER 6

Getting Ideas

After "How do you break into the business?" the second most-asked question I am asked is "Where do you get your ideas?" This whole book is about the former, so I'll address the latter question.

The answer is that I write about what I know, what I do, how I feel, where I've been, what I think. Some of my views, political and philosophical, are put into songs. I tell the stories of others who interest me.

Ideas for songs are much like any other ideas you have, and you know that a person cannot function in this society without having a few ideas as to what to do and where to go. Find something that interests you, then go ahead and write about it. Look for the opportunities and stay hot on their trail.

Everyone writes songs without even knowing it. A song is a story, a question, a message, or an emotion put into some framework. When you tell someone of an experience, an interesting person, or an emotion, you're actually writing a song.

Here are two song ideas: "There was an old man who lived up the road from us when I was a child . . ." and "I love my sweetheart very much, but. . . ."

In my travels I encounter many situations that arouse my curiosity. Why does so and so do that? What makes a woman act that way? Where is that child going? These questions interest me. They could become songs. If you will train yourself to look at and listen to what is going on around you, you will find almost unlimited ideas for songs. Condition yourself to think as a songwriter. Carry a notebook to write down clever lines you hear or an unusual thought you might have about someone or something. In the future those words or that idea might turn into a real "smasheroo."

As I was having a cup of coffee, I was spending the time thinking about ideas for songs. There were four or five thousand people mingling and milling around. I saw young hippie-type people, mature businessmen, old ladies, young women, young men. All of them were the beginning of a song.

Every person has his own peculiar way of walking and manner of dress and hair style. You might see an old man with a cane, a flowing white beard, a knapsack, and a book of poetry. In my estimation, he is a walking song. Try to create around this old gentleman a framework telling about the way he lives, thinks, what he does, where he goes.

You might see a beautiful young Oriental woman. Take note of the way she walks, what she appears to be drinking, whether she is in a hurry or taking her time, whether she is bored, depressed, or happy. She might suggest an idea for a song.

Just as you would not bring up a boring subject at a party, as you would not continue a trivial tale in a conversation, do not go on with a dull song idea expecting it to turn into a good song. Once while on a flight to one of my singing engagements, I found an interesting contest mentioned in a magazine. The rules of the contest were that you had to write an original opening line for a story. An example given was, "I was the only person in the world, and suddenly I heard a knock on the door."

Songwriters should think like that. I think that's a great opening line.

There's a Song Everywhere

The first song I wrote in Nashville was "Back Pocket Money." I was watching a recording session, and one of the musicians was talking to another about going to a ball game in Atlanta. "Boy, I've got to get my hands on some back pocket money." It struck me as humorous and catchy. The age-old problem of being low on cash turned into a good song, a hit.

One night my group, *The Storytellers*, and I worked at the

Preparing to hit the road.

Democratic National Convention in Miami Beach. After the show, I went back to my hotel and walked into the cocktail lounge. An old man was cleaning the tables while the bartender watched TV. "Ever had a drink of watermelon wine?" he asked. I had never heard of watermelon wine, and since we were the only two people in the table area of the bar, the old man started to philosophize.

Next morning, on my way back to Nashville, I wrote the song, "Old Dogs, Children, and Watermelon Wine." The song was a number one record for me, and I later realized I would never have written it had I not been aware of my profession and kept my ear keen to a new phrase or philosophy.

Right now, I am sitting in my office, looking out the window at a beautiful fir tree. During the Christmas season it is decorated, but now it isn't. For a while it was a highly regarded part of the landscape because it was lighted and tinseled and admired by everyone. Now it is just a common tree.

So, just outside the window, we have a situation for a song. We'll call it:

Have They Forgotten Me?
(A Tree)

Here I sit in a parking lot.
Time has passed and they've forgot.
Oh, I was once so bright and gay
But ah, that was another day.
At Christmas time I'm very high
But what do I do in mid-July?

I know this is a corny song and it wouldn't be a million-seller, but what I'm trying to say to you is that *there is a song outside your window*. There is a song in the people you meet. There is a song in the places you go. There is a song everywhere.

CHAPTER 7

Ways of Writing

There are so many ways to write a song it would be difficult to list them all. I do not want to give the impression that I am recommending any of these methods for you. However, it is well to know the methods other people use. The broader your exposure to proven methods, the better your likelihood of creating your own.

Dear . . .

I know one writer who always starts his songs with "Dearest Darling." This greeting is not a part of the body of the song; it is used to get his thoughts started in the right direction. As an example:

> Dearest Darling,
> I miss you so much since you've
> gone
> Please say you'll return to our home.

That's one way to approach your lyrics. Thinking you are writing a letter as you work on the lyrics makes you more aware of continuity, and it can overcome any traces of stage shyness you might have. After all, in a sense the writer of a song that eventually becomes popular is speaking to millions of people. That awareness can be a little frightening to a basically shy person and can prevent him from baring his inner emotions, the raw material for a highly successful song. If that person thinks of himself as communicating directly to a close friend or to a loved one with whom there is no need to guard his emotions, he can write a much more honest song than if he thinks primarily of his words going directly to the impersonal masses.

Think of a Word

Many people use the method employed by psychologists: "Say the first thing that comes into your mind when you hear the word 'love.'" Your reply could be "Joyce."

> Joyce, I love you and miss you every day.
> I've been going crazy since you went away.

Be careful. Don't rush into a line that starts off with a reference to unsingable sex acts.

A number of hit songs have been written by people who grabbed the spirit of the moment. They simply started singing words. A lot of songs have started out with absolutely no direction; then they were completed and given a title. It has been done and done well.

Collecting Ideas

Very similar to thinking of a word is the "first line" method. One writer has a file folder full of incomplete lyrics, songs not yet finished. He gets an idea for one line, a simple, direct statement that usually becomes the first line. If that basic idea is strong enough to generate a pattern of entertaining continuity, the song is completed; if not, it gets stashed away.

I know one lady who spends about an hour each week looking at the book titles in supermarkets. A lot of time and consideration go into the selection of a book title, and a title cannot be copyrighted—only the body of the work representing the book or the song. I am not recommending that you use this method, but the lady I have referred to makes a lot of money writing songs.

From Cars to People

It may surprise you to know that one famous country standard that expressed tender compliments, words of endearment, and an all-consuming fear of "losing you" was actually addressed to the writer's automobile. By transferring his emotions concerning that hard-earned car to the language we generally reserve for talking of love, he successfully enabled millions of people to identify his song with their own feelings.

Maybe you have a dog or horse or cat that you spend a lot of time with, petting and talking to it. You might find it easier to work out some of your song ideas in these "conversations" than by a more conventional manner.

One man I know is always under a railroad bridge when he writes. He is not under the bridge literally, he just puts himself there mentally to get the proper perspective of the world he writes about.

Using Headlines

Newspaper headlines have long been dependable song sources. Indeed, the purpose of songwriting and singing as practiced by medieval minstrels parallels the purpose of the news media today—communication of what's happening elsewhere and what has happened to certain people because of it. "The Death of Floyd Collins," "The Sinking of the Titanic," and "Little Kathy Fiscus" are old songs that came directly out of news accounts of tragedy.

Today such events bombard us so relentlessly that it takes a rare headline to spur a commercially successful song. But a lot of writers keep on trying, because every so often a song relating a recent calamity or news item will get recorded.

And TV, Too

Do you watch TV? What about the lines from the script of the shows? An actor says to an actress, "We have crossed a lot of bridges." Is this an idea for a song?

If you hear a line from a TV show or movie (or a radio or TV commercial) that generates an idea, you may want to jot it down. This technique has worked for other people; it can work for you.

See Two, See Them All

The most widely used method of country songwriting must be what we call "a play on words." Using an old cliché, you change words around until you have a different meaning. Example:

A bird in hand is worth two in a bed.

This example is not the cleverest I've heard, but it serves the purpose. Don't always say what you think; think what you say.

Keep in Touch

If you write a song that you think is good, keep it. Show it to someone occasionally. It may be ahead of its time and people aren't exactly ready for it, so don't discourage yourself because it is misunderstood the first time you present it. If you are convinced in your heart and mind that it is a good song, keep it.

Occasionally, I take a few days off, put on old clothes, let my beard grow, get in an old rental car or borrow a Jeep, and travel about the countryside looking at things. I sit in small cafes and talk to people who don't know that I'm a songwriter and just get the general drift of the way things are going in the country—the mood of the people. These are the people who listen to your music. You should not be interested in impressing other writers; you are interested in selling your songs to the public. If you know what these people—your public—are thinking, then you will be able to express what they are feeling, and your music will sell better.

Borrow

A lot of songs you hear are not really songs. They are what we in the business call recitations or song poems. How can a person write a song without music?

The answer is simple: You already "own" thousands of melodies or tunes.

After a copyright expires, a song falls into public domain, or P.D., which means that it belongs to everyone. Anyone who wants to use it may do so without paying for its use or being sued for song stealing. Public domain songs are on file at the Library of Congress, mainly old songs whose author or composer is unknown. In recent years, several big hit songs were recitations with a P.D. melody played behind them.

If you have a great poem you would like to see recorded, try the following method. Place one of your favorite instrumental albums on the stereo, and read your poem to the background music. If your poem is highly dramatic, you may want a selection that is fast and exciting. If it is a sad poem, you will want to find a musical selection in keeping with its mood.

By placing your home tape recorder microphone near the sound of the music coming from your record player and by reading your poem into the microphone at the same time, you can get a performance of your recitation that sounds pretty good. It is great fun to have a selection of your song poems on hand for presentation at parties or family gatherings. You can also use these tapes as a demonstration presentation of your work.

To find out if the music is in P.D., look on the back of the album jacket. If it states, "Arr. by _____ (person's name)," where the publisher credits are usually listed, it probably is in P.D.

Remember, you need to use songs known to be old. An arrangement of a P.D. song can be copyrighted, and the writer is due all normal royalties from that particular work; so if you use a modern artist's arrangement of an old tune, you will have to pay royalties. However, it does not mean he has any claim to the original melody, which is still in P.D.

This may be stretching the use of public domain a bit, but some songs that have been recorded were not written by any known person. These songs are a product of research. In these instances we have a P.D. melody and a poem by an unknown author. If we put the two together and make a recording, what do we have? The answer is simple. We—or whoever compiled the two—have an original work that can be copyrighted and on which all normal royalties are paid. I suppose we could call that "How to Write Without Really Writing."

Combining song and recitation is not rare at all. The verse, chorus, or any line in the song can be spoken. To write a spoken part into one of your songs, simply put *"spoken"* before the line that you want read instead of sung.

Here is an illustration:

> When the dew is on the roses
> And the wind is in your hair
> SPOKEN:
> Seek the spirit of the wind
> For I'll be there.

The music you have written or selected for your song will continue to carry the melody of your song, even when you have chosen to speak a few lines.

In looking through collections of American poems, I have come across several that my friends have written into their songs. If you find a good poem to set to music, and if you have found it in some obscure publication with the author listed as "Unknown," take credit for it. There is something to be said for a talent that can recognize a poem that would be suitable to set to music. Some of the greatest songwriters have done this successfully.

Finally, if you do not have a great speaking voice, ask a friend with a good voice to read for you. I can assure you he or she would be flattered by that request.

CHAPTER 8

Rhyme

Songwriting is a first cousin to writing poetry. Music and poetry are so closely related that some writers have had volumes of their song lyrics published.

One of the first things many people think of when they think of poetry is rhyme. Although not all poetry rhymes, it is important for the beginning songwriter to master the skill of rhyming.

Kinds of Rhyme Patterns

Some authorities may have definitions that are more technical, but I have summarized three of the most frequently used rhyme patterns for songwriting in a little verse of sorts:

> Rhyme every line,
> Skip a line and rhyme,
> Or rhyme within the line.

That little verse also illustrates another form of rhyme pattern—false rhyme. By that I mean that *line* and *rhyme* don't really rhyme, but they sound enough alike to suggest that a rhyme has been made. They are not an exact rhyme, like *moon* and *June*, *hear* and *fear*, *shake* and *bake*, but they are close enough to create the feeling of rhyme. Some false rhymes are closer than others: *too* and *few* are not exact, but they are closer than *hiding* and *lying*.

One of the purposes of rhyme is to tie the lines of the song together. Songwriting and poetry are tighter forms of literary art than short stories and novels. While the meter of the lines (the pattern of the accents on the words) helps bring about this tightness, the repetition of sound (rhyme) is a highly creative contribution.

Let's look at an example of "rhyme every line":

> She went to Mexico.
> I told her not to go.
> Next day she returned
> With the Spanish she had learned.

This pattern is widely used, but sometimes it doesn't give the writer enough freedom to bring in as many new words as he may need to expand the idea on which his song is built.

That is why "skip a line and rhyme" comes in handy, for it takes four lines instead of two to tie up a specific thought. Let me illustrate:

> She went to Mexico.
> She never did return.
> I sought her high and low
> With some Spanish I had learned.

"Rhyme within the line" (for example, "did she GO to Mexico?") is a handy little tool for adding extra punch to a line. Some songs combine the rhyme-within-a-line technique with an every-other-line pattern to give a very interesting effect. One of the strongest illustrations is Bill Anderson's song "Quits." Take a look at or listen to those lyrics sometime, and you'll really get the feel of this technique at its best.

If you use rhyme-within-the-line in a way that doesn't detract from the message of the song—if it's not too obvious, that is—it can have a big impact on the total song. If you are obvious about it, or cute and artsy, a lot of people won't take the song very seriously.

To Rhyme or Not to Rhyme

Some songs have no rhyme at all. Such a one could be:

> I love you more than whiskey,
> I love you more than wine,
> But these are so much easier
> To hold, don't you see.

While that particular illustration has little hope in the Grammy race, I want to stress that the rhyme-less technique is not a lack of a technique. Rather, it is difficult to tie the lines of a song together by the use of unrhymed words alone. Until you get to the point in your songwriting that you have made tremendous headway in mastering subtleties of word usage so that you consistently build up rhythm and continuity in your writing, I would suggest that you make use of all the rhyme techniques before you try to write unrhymed songs. I'm not saying don't write them; I'm just saying you should take each step as it comes and not be too eager to find shortcuts. There aren't any.

The more you know about the rules and tools and the better you are at using them, the more capable you then become of bending and even breaking them to adjust to your individuality. So work at it. Learn rhymes and how to use them.

Be Consistent

It doesn't really matter how you handle rhyme in a song, but it is a good idea to be consistent. If you use a certain pattern in the first verse, use the same pattern (although not necessarily the same rhyming sound) in the following verses. Change the pattern for the bridge if you wish, but if you use different lyrics with each bridge, use the same rhyme pattern each time. If you don't, you're likely to have an assortment of disjoined pieces instead of a well-knit song.

Time to Rhyme

Since not all songwriters are clever with rhymes, it's a good idea to get help. Many dictionaries have a "vocabulary of rhymes" in the back, there are complete rhyming dictionaries, and *Roget's Thesaurus* is a classic reference book for anyone dealing with the English language. You will find it highly beneficial to acquire the reference aids that fit your personal taste and needs. Many are available, and most of them offer a deeper dip into the technicalities of word usage than we have space for here, but I do want to provide a brief list of rhymes that can be helpful to you as you write. Don't for a minute consider this a complete listing, but perhaps it will help broaden your understanding of rhymes.

For instance, in looking for a word ending with an *ab* sound, you can choose from bab, blab, cab, crab, dab, drab, gab, grab, mab, nab, scab, slab, stab, and tab. Country writers may choose to exercise their poetic license and refer to the long-eared small-game animal by the shortened name of *rab*. Ray Stevens had a lot of fun and made a lot of money with that same rhyming sound. *Ahab* and *Arab* were his key words.

My point is that a lot of times looking at a prepared rhyming list can spur your mind into finding left-field possibilities that may fill the verbal hole in your song with just the right word.

Among the words on the long list of those that rhyme with the *ade* sound are aid, blade, braid, fade, glade, grade, jade, laid, made, maid, raid, shade, spade, suede, degrade, evade, grenade, invade, parade, persuade, stockade, tirade, escapade, marmalade, masquerade, renegade, paid, played, obeyed, and weighed. A song idea could go in any of many directions from one of those words at the end of a line that needs a rhyme.

And so it is with the *ain* sound: brain, chain, crane, Dane, drain, feign, gain, grain, lane, main, mane, pain, pane, plain, plane, rain, reign, sane, slain, Spain, sprain, stain, train, twain, vain, vane, vein, wane, abstain, airplane, attain, campaign, champagne, complain, contain, detain, disdain, domain, explain, humane, inane, insane, maintain, obtain, ordain, pertain, profane, refrain, regain, remain, restrain, retain, sustain, urbane, ascertain, entertain, and hurricane.

For *ent:* bent, cent, dent, lent, meant, rent, scent, sent, spent, tent, vent, went, absent, ascent, cement, content, indent, intent, invent, lament, present, prevent, accident, ailment, argument, banishment, complement, compliment, confident, detriment, different, document, element, eloquent, eminent, evident, excellent, government, instrument, monument, negligent, nourishment, orient, ornament, permanent, punishment, represent, tenement, violent, wonderment, acknowledgement, astonishment, benevolent, experiment, intelligent, irreverent, and magnificent.

Some sounds provide less choice. For example, hardly anything rhymes with *Barb* except *garb*. Country writers have problems finding something other than *blue* to rhyme with *you*. Brew, chew, clue, crew, cue, drew, due, few, flew, blue, grew, hew, Jew, knew, new, pew, screw, stew, strew, sue, through, and interview are among the possibilities, although some are obviously a little left-field.

Love is another toughie, not only because it comes up so often, but also because after *dove* and *above* you have little more than glove, shove, turtledove, and unlove.

There is no way we can get into all the details of rhyme here. I suggest that you pursue the subject as diligently as you should pursue chord progressions and the other elements of melody construction.

CHAPTER 9

Meter

We've talked about rhyme, so now let's talk about meter, which is one of the most basic and important elements of a song. Meter is—in my own quaint definition—rhythm. It is the natural order of things. One and one is two—that's meter. Both eyes blink at the same time—that's meter. Walking is meter—clomp, clomp, clomp, clomp. However, clomp, clomp, click, clomp—that is out of meter. It is not the natural order of things.

In the construction of good meter, the primary building block is the syllable. For the purposes of songwriting and for the sake of poetic license (which occasionally winks an eye at the technicalities of proper grammatical constructions), our syllable is simply one sound.

As an example of good meter, I have used the children's rhyme "Mary Had a Little Lamb." In the name of *Mary*, we have two sounds or syllables—Mar-y. Take a look at the poem illustrated here:

> Mary had a little lamb,
> Its fleece was white as snow.
> Everywhere that Mary went
> The lamb was sure to go.

Now, in the place of the words, I have indicated the number of syllables as follows:

> Line One: (seven syllables)
> Line Two: (six syllables)
> Line Three: (seven syllables)
> Line Four: (six syllables)

Thus, our meter is 7, 6, 7, 6.

Surprising phone call at the office.

As an exercise, disregard the original lyric and, for each sylla-ble indicated, substitute a word or syllable of your own. By doing so, you will have created a well-metered, original verse. Following is my own example, using the illustrated meter as my basis:

> Char-lie was a jol-ly guy, (7)
> He ne-ver took a drink. (6)
> If he took a drink at all (7)
> It made him want to dance. (6)

You can easily see the natural order of this meter. Explaining meter is almost as difficult as telling someone how to walk. To help, take this exercise, fill in your own words, and write your own story, just as I have written the story of Charlie who wanted to dance when he had a drink. Then I think it will be easier for you to grasp the meaning of meter, of rhythm, and of the natural order of the way a song should be. In contrast, here is an example of a verse that does *not* meet the requirements of meter:

Char-lie was a ver-y jol-ly guy, (9)
He ne-ver took a drink. (6)
If he took a drink at all (7)
It made him want to dance. (6)

What is wrong here? Obviously there are too many syllables. The first line contains an extra word, which makes it two syllables too long.

A good way to learn what meter is about would be to read some simple poetry. All of the Mother Goose rhymes are metered very well and distinctly. Once meter is completely understood, you will learn how words can be stretched or abbreviated, added or eliminated to achieve good meter. Here, too, your melody can aid you in stretching words to cover the additional beats of time to achieve the well-metered lines.

Let me emphasize that one should first completely understand the rules of songwriting before deciding whether altering a rule (or adjusting the natural order of things) is necessary. Good meter makes a song much more comfortable to listen to, much more comprehensible, and, we hope, more successful. The more naturally this is achieved, the more comfortable it will sound.

CHAPTER 10

Music for the Words

S ome people may argue this point, but I personally believe that the lyrics are what make or break a good song. They must say something and say it in an entertaining way. At the same time, we ARE talking about songs, and songs mean music. And that means melody.

There's no way we can really do justice to the techniques of musical composition in a book of this nature; but the basics are quite simple, at least for those who have a natural instinct for music. Someone whose instincts for communication lie elsewhere would be more interested in learning to write a novel or something other than songs.

Take advantage of all the educational opportunities related to music that you have access to—piano or other musical instrument lessons, band or chorus lessons in school, or even formal courses in music theory and musicology if you want. But your best, and most accessible, source of musical education is simply listening to today's music.

Melody-building

Elsewhere in this book I refer to meter and the pattern of accents in the words you use in your songs. I don't have to tell you that rhythm is the very foundation of melody and that the meter pattern of these accents naturally contributes to the general direction your songs take.

I learned melody construction as a child listening to country songs on the radio. As I began to get ideas for songs, it was natural for me to use the melody progression of the songs I already knew. As I got better at putting the words together, I got better at rearranging the melodic elements with more originality.

After all, there are only twelve tones in the musical scale (A, B, C, D, E, F, and G, and five halftones—the sharps and flats). With these twelve notes and tones and half-tones we have a pretty broad range of possibilities. Every song, tune, melody, concerto, tone-poem, or symphony is constructed with those same twelve tones.

Keep the Tune Simple

Since I am involved with country music, I know more about it than any other type. Even though the basic elements of melody construction are fundamental to all music, the emphasis given to certain aspects may vary from one kind to another. Country music thrives on simple melodies. A certain amount of sophistication and experimentation may have its place, but you should try to make your melodies simple enough for the average person to be able to hum or whistle to himself as he goes about his daily doings. He's the one who buys your songs!

Basically, situations suggest melodies. A train wreck, for instance, suggests a rumbling sort of exciting sound, while a daisy waving in a meadow breeze suggests an altogether different melody. Somewhere between the daisy and the train wreck, between "Look out!" and "I love you," there is a melody for your song.

As a preliminary step, I suggest you talk the line in a melodic tone. Try it with a familiar line such as:

> Now is the time for all good men
> to come to the aid of their country.

Repeat that familiar line to yourself while keeping your ear alert to changes of inflection that would translate in musical terms to changes in melody. Read aloud the Pledge of Allegiance to the Flag. Then compare the tone to the reading of some lines from "The Raven": "Once upon a midnight dreary while I pondered weak and weary. . . ." Use your own favorite lines of prose and poetry. Try singing "Good morning!" or "Good evening!" or "Hi, there!"

See if you find a melodic sound to each that is different from the other. When you have interesting ideas, jot them down. Then when you sit down to write, depending on your mood, pick one of these lines to work with and begin to hum the phrase over in your mind.

Start with Parodies

The writing of parodies is a good method for the beginning writer to use. Although *parody* often has a comical connotation, that isn't always the case.

Take a tune you know well and write new words for it. This gives you a pattern for your work, not entirely unlike the way a "paint-by-number" set gives you the opportunity to construct recognizeable images on canvas by following a predrawn outline.

To show you what I mean, here's a little verse I jotted down to go with the tune of "Red River Valley":

> Oh, I know that the days can be lonely
> 'Cause I've surely had my share of them
> It's a shame that I think of you only
> And that you only care about him.

Doctoring a Melody

Next, you can take a melody you know and "doctor" it. Where a note goes up, take it down, or just change it any way you want. A lot of writers will wince when I say this, but that's basically what we do, whether or not we realize or admit it.

Remember, those twelve different tones don't seem to give you a lot of room to play, but as you become more familiar with them and their relationship to one other, you will be surprised at how you can continue to create original melodies.

Don't Let It Scare You

Music must have originated with those who had no knowledge of music at all. They didn't know it could be written; they just did it naturally.

Don't be frightened about melodies or songs. Construct them in a manner that suits and entertains you. If you are able to entertain yourself with your songs, chances are you will be able to entertain someone else, too.

Finding a Collaborator

Let's suppose you have a song—a song poem—but you don't write melodies. What do you do then? Songwriting is much like any other hobby; you don't realize how many people are involved in it until you get involved in it yourself. If you become interested in writing songs, you will find a lot of people interested in the same thing.

If you have written what you consider to be some good song poems, I think you should acquaint yourself with what is going on musically in your hometown. You don't have to be concerned with Los Angeles, New York, Chicago, or Nashville unless you live there. Your own hometown is the place to start.

As you meet people who are interested in songwriting and in playing music and getting involved in the music business, you'll find some who play and sing quite well and others who also write song poems. So the first person you have to convince with your song poems is someone who writes music and can put music to your words. Then, of course, you become co-writers. In Nashville each co-writer takes 50 percent of the song.

Your co-writer, especially if he or she plays guitar and sings, probably has a few original melodies running around in his head. Maybe he'll put a melody to your song and make you a tape of it; then you'll have it for presentation.

Paying for Help

Of course, if you don't do your own melodies and can't find anyone who plays guitar or does music, there are people who claim that—for a price—they will put melodies to your songs and send you a demonstration record. I write my own melodies. I make up a song's melody at the same time I'm doing its lyrics because the lyrics say something to me about melody.

I'm not much in favor of sending songs off to a stranger; you're writing off to people you have never met and hardly know. It's sort of like sending one of your children off to a school you haven't investigated. My songs are my children, and I keep them at home and look after them there.

CHAPTER 11

Revising Your Song

I f songwriters were a violent sort, the subject of songwriting could be dangerously controversial. A lot of good writers believe so strongly in first instincts while writing a song that they never change a word or a line once they decide that word or line is the right one. On the other hand, as a matter of routine some writers go back to songs they have written a day or so earlier to beef up the melody, the lyrics, or both with the benefit of afterthought.

In the same way I am trying to be objective, so I am not going to tell you that either approach is the best way. You may find that in your particular case a lot of rewriting gets you off the path along which your original idea was going. If that's true, you would do well to train your mind to get as deep as possible into the mood and message of your idea while you are engaged in the initial writing. If you don't do this, some of your best thoughts may never find a home on paper.

In contrast, conditioning your thinking to an "Oh-I'll-just-jot-down-the-main-gist-of-this-idea-now-and-then-polish-it-up-when-I-have-more-time" attitude can lead to laziness. Truthfully, though, the degree of danger to your craft as a songwriter depends entirely upon the degree of your interest, intention, and dedication.

If you want to pursue songwriting only as an occasional hobby to get your mind off everyday hassles, practically any approach comfortable to you will suffice. If you want to buy divisions of rolling Middle Tennessee farmland with song royalties, I suggest you develop a mental discipline in keeping with the serious nature of making a living in any sort of enterprise.

OLD DOGS, CHILDREN, AND WATERMELON WINE

HOLW OLD DO YOU THINK I AM? HE SAID
I SAID, WELL ~~I DON'T~~ *I didn't know*
HE SAID, I TURNED SIXTY-FIVE ABOUT ELEVEN MONTHS AGO
I WAS SITTIN' IN MIAMI, POURIN' BLENDED WHISKEY DOWN
WHEN THIS OLD GREY BLACK GENTLEMAN WAS CLEANIN' UP THE LOUNGE.

THERE WASN'T ANYONE AROUND 'CEPT THIS OLD MAN AND ME
THE GUY WHO RAN THE BAR WAS WATCHIN' IRONSIDES ON T.V.
UNINVITED HE SAT DOWN AND OPENED UP HIS MIND
ON OLD DOGS AND CHILDREN AND WATERMELON WINE

EVER HAD A DRINK OF WATERMELON ~~W~~ *wine he said*
HE TOLD ME ALL ABOUT IT THOUGH I DIDN'T ANSWER BACK
AIN'T BUT THREE THINGS IN THIS WORLD THAT'S WORTH A SOLITARY DIME
BUT OLD DOGS, CHILDREN AND WATERMELON WINE

HE SAID WOMEN THINK ABOUT THEYSELVES WHEN MENFOLK AIN'T AROUND
AND FRIENDS ARE HARD TO FIND WHEN THEY DISCOVER THAT YOU'RE DOWN
HE SAID I TRIED IT ALL WHEN I WAS YOUNG AND IN MY NATURAL PRIME
NOW IT'S OLD DOGS, CHILDREN AND WATERMELON WINE.

Old dogs CARE ABOUT YOU EVEN WHEN YOU MAKE MISTAKES
GOD BLESS LITTLE CHILDREN WHILE THEY'RE STILL TOO YOUNG TO HATE
WHEN HE MOVED AWAY, I FOUND MY PEN AND COPIED DOWN THAT LINE
'BOUT OLD DOGS AND CHILDREN AND WATERMELON WINE.

I HAD TO CATCH A PLANE UP TO ATLANTA ~~~~ *the next day*
AS I LEFT FOR MY ROOM I SAW HIM PICKIN' UP MY CHANGE
THAT NIGHT I DREAMED IN PEACEFUL SLEEP OF SHADY SUMMERTIME
OF OLD DOGS AND CHILDREN AND WATERMELON WINE.

Ravishing Ruby

Ravishing Ruby she sleeps in
a bunk out back —
Her days and nights are
filled with dreams of a man
manne Smiling Jack —
That was her daddy's name
That all she ever knew
Ravishing Ruby ~~she~~ ain't got
time for ~~man~~ guys like you
and me —

~~She web~~ Ravishing Ruby, believes
anything you say — Just like
her daddy said — said he'd
be back some day
waitin on ole Smiley Jack
He'll come Rollin by —
She wants to see him — she
wants to lose him
Either way — dead or alive

You probably have guessed that my personal approach to rewriting is somewhere in the middle. To illustrate, I'm going to show you the original longhand drafts of two of my songs, "Old Dogs, Children and Watermelon Wine" and "Ravishing Ruby."

Actually, the very first version of "Old Dogs" was written on a sick bag aboard an airplane. It is now part of the collection of original song manuscripts hanging in the lobby of ASCAP, The American Society of Composers, Authors, and Publishers, in Nashville. The one I have included here is the first draft of the finished version. Even at that stage, you'll see I changed my mind several times about the way the song should go.

On the other hand, you can see that "Ravishing Ruby" had a different sort of flow to it while I was writing.

I would recommend the ASCAP lyrics display as an important aid in learning the craft of songwriting. Studying the work of other writers is helpful in giving you a firm footing to work from into directions of your own, and being able to see the early corrections and changes on songs with which you are familiar will help strengthen that knowledge. Another good place to study is the library of the Country Music Foundation in the lower and top levels of the Country Music Hall of Fame and Museum in Nashville. It contains a lot of basic information.

Sometimes the circumstances permit little rewriting. Johnny Rodriguez and I had been working on "Answer to Your Letter," but we did not have the song far enough along to use it in a session he had scheduled for his first album for Phonogram-Mercury. However, the song just wouldn't get off our minds. So early on the morning of the session, we got back on it, wrote the last verse, and headed straight for the studio, where he recorded it. There was almost no time for any second-thinking or rewriting.

All in all, flexibility probably should be the key. Put as much effort as you can into your songs when you first write them, but don't be afraid to make changes that would improve them. Absolutely refusing to make any changes is as bad as knowing while you're writing a song that you're going to change it around some, from force of habit if for no other reason.

CHAPTER 12

Communicating

Once you have your melody, you have to communicate it to others. To do this you have to hum or play a musical instrument. I don't believe I know a single songwriter who cannot play some kind of musical instrument. If you don't know how, learn.

Pick Out the Melody

After only a few minutes of practice almost anyone can pick out a melody note by note on a piano. If you have an idea for a melody you think could be successful—something associated with some pleasant or unpleasant memory, some childhood recollection—I would recommend you get access to a musical instrument, preferably a piano because it is the most nearly universal instrument. With a little patience, you will find you can pick out the melody to the song you have in mind and communicate it to others.

Hum It to Someone

If you don't play an instrument or can't get the use of one, you still have a recourse: You can always hum.

Unfortunately, a tape recording of you humming into a microphone may not be taken seriously by a publisher. So what you should do is hum your melody to someone who can play it on an instrument or write it down. Remember the old story of the intoxicated man who stumbled into the bar, walked over to the piano player, and said, "Hey! Do you know what the old cat did in the shavin's?" And the piano player answered, "No, but if you'll hum a few bars, I'll try to play it."

Once you have your music written or on tape, you can submit it to a publisher or take it to someone who writes music and can make you a leadsheet (sheet music). You then have your melody in workable form for presentation.

Don't Be Too Ambitious

If you are interested in writing music, you probably already have some idea of how you think it should sound. However, unless you have much experience, leave the arrangements to the producer. You will find that when musicians actually perform music, unusual things sometimes "happen" as each individual "feels" the song. It may not "happen" that exact way in your own head.

Make your presentation basic and uncomplicated, much as you would hum "The Star-Spangled Banner." You don't hear the drums rolling or the bugles blaring and the fills. (The fills are those additions in an arrangement that keep the flow of the music smooth and unbroken.) For instance, hum the first line of "The Star-Spangled Banner." You will note the break, or slight pause, between "see" and "by the dawn's early light." The arranger or producer would bring in some instrument at this point as "fill" so that this pause would not be so clearly felt.

It's the Song That Counts

There's no point in making your presentation complicated or in spending thousands of dollars having your song made ready for presentation to a publisher or an artist. I will tell you the way we operate in Nashville, and I believe they operate the same way in other places, too. Publishers and artists everywhere are looking for the same thing—hit songs.

If a publisher or artist firmly believes you have a hit song, he won't care if you sing it a cappella (without musical accompaniment), if you sing while accompanying yourself on an African drum, or if you had Elvis singing it on a demonstration tape. Publishers and artists pay no attention to how a song is presented as long as they can get the message and they think it's a hit. They are professional people who know—or, on occasion, think they know—a hit song when they hear it or a great idea for a hit song when exposed to it.

CHAPTER 13

Selecting Colleagues

If you become a successful songwriter, your publisher will no doubt be associated with you. So when you walk into a publisher's office with some songs, you must consider that this man is sizing you up. He's deciding if he wants to share his time, career, office procedure, and method of operation with you for many years to come. It takes time to develop a writer.

Presenting your songs to a publisher is not unlike applying for a job. It may not be the nicest thing to say of the music industry, but your physical appearance can play an important part in your personal acceptance, which is essential to the acceptance of your work. Despite the trends of the times, there are people who are turned off by a shaggy, sloppy appearance; and some of these people are in a position to help you. You do yourself a disservice to deliberately provoke their distaste when it would involve only a little more effort to appear neater and more pleasant. You are probably thinking that I refer mostly to hair length, but that's just part of it; a dirty shirt offends many people. If you insist on "free thinking" in the matter of dress and appearance, you have to extend that same freedom to people who choose to avoid you.

Wouldn't it be terrible if, after spending so much time writing those tremendous songs, when you presented yourself to the people who listen to them, they decided that, even though your songs are good, the money that could be made from them would not be enough to make it worth tolerating your presence? Keep in mind that you must be neat. Present yourself intelligently, respectfully, and humbly.

Song Sharks

It seems the greatest fear a writer has is that someone is going to steal one of his or her songs.

First of all, I would like to tell you my personal opinion of song stealing: I don't think it is a very prevalent thing. In fact, I said on one occasion that if someone had wanted to steal one of my songs when I was an amateur songwriter—when I was first getting started—it would have been the greatest compliment in the world, that the shark would have thought enough of my song to steal it.

Like any other professional, a writer needs confidence in what he is doing. Songwriting is not one song anyway. If you're going to make it a profession, it's song after song after song. So if someone steals one and makes a few thousand dollars, you know you're writing stuff that's worth stealing. Then you have the license to go ahead and write songs for as long as you live—because that early song was good enough to steal.

I wouldn't consider stealing a song. I'm like everybody else in the world, certainly every other songwriter. I'm prejudiced. I think my songs are better than what I could pick up and steal. I think most writers feel that way.

Protecting Yourself

The music publishing business is a very legitimate business, especially in Nashville, which I think is one of the most honest towns in the world. Here we're getting into something I want to talk about, but I don't want you to take it to your lawyer and say, "This is what Tom T. Hall does and I have to do it, too," because he may give you different advice.

However, here is a tip which may help protect your songs if you have the lyrics typewritten and recorded on a cassette tape. Before you show your songs to anyone, take a copy of the cassette to the post office and mail it to yourself via registered mail. I always did this early in my career; it gave me a sense of well-being.

I know a lot of people say this doesn't work and that it doesn't protect the song. But if I have to go before a judge or a jury to defend my song and I have a package in my hand with a government seal on it, dated and mailed to me, I can make my point if I open it in the courtroom and inside is a song exactly like the one that's on the market.

I know this is not a surefire way to protect a song. But if someone wanted to steal a song and knew you had mailed it to yourself through the registered mail some time ago, he might be a little more reluctant to get entangled in it.

APPLICATION FOR COPYRIGHT REGISTRATION
for a
Work of the Performing Arts

FORM PA

UNITED STATES COPYRIGHT OFFICE
LIBRARY OF CONGRESS
WASHINGTON, D.C. 20559

HOW TO APPLY FOR COPYRIGHT REGISTRATION:

- **First:** Read the information on this page to make sure Form PA is the correct application for your work.

- **Second:** Open out the form by pulling this page to the left. Read through the detailed instructions before starting to complete the form.

- **Third:** Complete spaces 1-4 of the application, then turn the entire form over and, after reading the instructions for spaces 5-9, complete the rest of your application. Use typewriter or print in dark ink. Be sure to sign the form at space 8.

- **Fourth:** Detach your completed application from these instructions and send it with the necessary deposit of the work (see below) to: Register of Copyrights, Library of Congress, Washington, D.C. 20559. Unless you have a Deposit Account in the Copyright Office, your application and deposit must be accompanied by a check or money order for $10, payable to: *Register of Copyrights.*

WHEN TO USE FORM PA: Form PA is the appropriate application to use for copyright registration covering works of the performing arts. Both published and unpublished works can be registered on Form PA.

WHAT IS A "WORK OF THE PERFORMING ARTS"? This category includes works prepared for the purpose of being "performed" directly before an audience or indirectly "by means of any device or process." Examples of works of the performing arts are: (1) musical works, including any accompanying words. (2) dramatic works, including any accompanying music. (3) pantomimes and choreographic works, and (4) motion pictures and other audiovisual works **Note:** This category does not include sound recordings, which should be registered on Form SR For more information about copyright in sound recordings, see the reverse side of this sheet

DEPOSIT TO ACCOMPANY APPLICATION: An application for copyright registration must be accompanied by a deposit representing the entire work for which registration is to be made. The following are the general deposit requirements as set forth in the statute:

Unpublished work: Deposit one complete copy or phonorecord.

Published work: Deposit two complete copies or phonorecords of the best edition.

Work first published outside the United States: Deposit one complete copy or phonorecord of the first foreign edition.

Contribution to a collective work: Deposit one complete copy or phonorecord of the best edition of the collective work.

These general deposit requirements may vary in particular situations. For further information about the specific deposit requirements for particular types of works of the performing arts, see the reverse side of this sheet. For general information about copyright deposit, write to the Copyright Office.

THE COPYRIGHT NOTICE: For published works, the law provides that a copyright notice in a specified form "shall be placed on all publicly distributed copies from which the work can be visually perceived." Use of the copyright notice is the responsibility of the copyright owner and does not require advance permission from the Copyright Office. The required form of the notice for copies generally consists of three elements: (1) the symbol "©", or the word "Copyright", or the abbreviation "Copr."; (2) the year of first publication; and (3) the name of the owner of copyright. For example: "© 1978 Alexander Hollenius". The notice is to be affixed to the copies "in such manner and location as to give reasonable notice of the claim of copyright." Unlike the law in effect before 1978, the new copyright statute provides procedures for correcting errors in the copyright notice, and even for curing the omission of the notice. However, a failure to comply with the notice requirements may still result in the loss of some copyright protection and, unless corrected within five years, in the complete loss of copyright. For further information about the copyright notice, see the reverse side of this sheet. For additional information concerning the copyright notice and the procedures for correcting errors or omissions, write to the Copyright Office.

DURATION OF COPYRIGHT: For works that were created after the effective date of the new statute (January 1, 1978), the basic copyright term will be the life of the author and fifty years after the author's death. For works made for hire, and for certain anonymous and pseudonymous works, the duration of copyright will be 75 years from publication or 100 years from creation, whichever is shorter. These same terms of copyright will generally apply to works that had been created before 1978 but had not been published or copyrighted before that date. For further information about the duration of copyright, including the terms of copyrights already in existence before 1978, write for Circular R15a.

FORM PA

UNITED STATES COPYRIGHT OFFICE

REGISTRATION NUMBER
PA   PAU

EFFECTIVE DATE OF REGISTRATION

....
(Month)   (Day)   (Year)

DO NOT WRITE ABOVE THIS LINE. IF YOU NEED MORE SPACE, USE CONTINUATION SHEET (FORM PA/CON)

(1) Title

TITLE OF THIS WORK:

NATURE OF THIS WORK: (See instructions)

PREVIOUS OR ALTERNATIVE TITLES:

(2) Author(s)

IMPORTANT: Under the law, the "author" of a "work made for hire" is generally the employer, not the employee (see instructions). If any part of this work was "made for hire" check "Yes" in the space provided, give the employer (or other person for whom the work was prepared) as "Author" of that part, and leave the space for dates blank.

1

NAME OF AUTHOR:

Was this author's contribution to the work a "work made for hire"?   Yes   No

DATES OF BIRTH AND DEATH:
Born .... Died ....
(Year)   (Year)

AUTHOR'S NATIONALITY OR DOMICILE:
Citizen of .... } or { Domiciled in ....
(Name of Country)   (Name of Country)

WAS THIS AUTHOR'S CONTRIBUTION TO THE WORK:
Anonymous?   Yes   No
Pseudonymous?   Yes   No
If the answer to either of these questions is "Yes," see detailed instructions attached.

AUTHOR OF: (Briefly describe nature of this author's contribution)

2

NAME OF AUTHOR:

Was this author's contribution to the work a "work made for hire"?   Yes   No

DATES OF BIRTH AND DEATH:
Born .... Died ....
(Year)   (Year)

AUTHOR'S NATIONALITY OR DOMICILE:
Citizen of .... } or { Domiciled in ....
(Name of Country)   (Name of Country)

WAS THIS AUTHOR'S CONTRIBUTION TO THE WORK:
Anonymous?   Yes   No
Pseudonymous?   Yes   No
If the answer to either of these questions is "Yes," see detailed instructions attached.

AUTHOR OF: (Briefly describe nature of this author's contribution)

3

NAME OF AUTHOR:

Was this author's contribution to the work a "work made for hire"?   Yes   No

DATES OF BIRTH AND DEATH:
Born .... Died ....
(Year)   (Year)

AUTHOR'S NATIONALITY OR DOMICILE:
Citizen of .... } or { Domiciled in ....
(Name of Country)   (Name of Country)

WAS THIS AUTHOR'S CONTRIBUTION TO THE WORK:
Anonymous?   Yes   No
Pseudonymous?   Yes   No
If the answer to either of these questions is "Yes," see detailed instructions attached.

AUTHOR OF: (Briefly describe nature of this author's contribution)

(3) Creation and Publication

YEAR IN WHICH CREATION OF THIS WORK WAS COMPLETED:

Year..........
(This information must be given in all cases.)

DATE AND NATION OF FIRST PUBLICATION:

Date ....
(Month)   (Day)   (Year)
Nation ....
(Name of Country)
(Complete this block ONLY if this work has been published.)

(4) Claimant(s)

NAME(S) AND ADDRESS(ES) OF COPYRIGHT CLAIMANT(S):

TRANSFER: (If the copyright claimant(s) named here in space 4 are different from the author(s) named in space 2, give a brief statement of how the claimant(s) obtained ownership of the copyright.)

- Complete all applicable spaces (numbers 5-9) on the reverse side of this page
- Follow detailed instructions attached   • Sign the form at line 8

DO NOT WRITE HERE

Page 1 of .... pages

HOW TO FILL OUT FORM PA

Specific Instructions for Spaces 1-4

- The line-by-line instructions on this page are keyed to the spaces on the first page of Form PA, printed opposite.
- Please read through these instructions before you start filling out your application, and refer to the specific instructions for each space as you go along.

SPACE 1: TITLE

- **Title of this Work:** Every work submitted for copyright registration must be given a title that is capable of identifying that particular work. If the copies or phonorecords of the work bear a title (or an identifying phrase that could serve as a title), transcribe its wording completely and exactly on the application. Remember that indexing of the registration and future identification of the work will depend on the information you give here.

  If the work you are registering is an entire "collective work" (such as a collection of plays or songs), give the over-all title of the collection. If you are registering one or more individual contributions to a collective work, give the title of

each contribution, followed by the title of the collection. Example: " 'A Song for Elinda' in *Old and New Ballads for Old and New People.*"

- **Nature of this Work:** Briefly describe the general nature or character of the work being registered for copyright. Examples: "Music"; "Song Lyrics"; "Words and Music"; "Drama"; "Musical Play"; "Choreography"; "Pantomime"; "Motion Picture"; "Audiovisual Work".
- **Previous or Alternative Titles:** Complete this space if there are any additional titles for the work under which someone searching for the registration might be likely to look, or under which a document pertaining to the work might be recorded.

SPACE 2: AUTHORS

- **General Instructions:** First decide, after reading these instructions, who are the "authors" of this work for copyright purposes. Then, unless the work is a "collective work" (see below), give the requested information about every "author" who contributed any appreciable amount of copyrightable matter to this version of the work. If you need further space, use the attached Continuation Sheet and, if n·· ··v, request additional Continuation Sheets (Form PA/CON).
- **Who is the "Auth... :"** Unless the work was "made for hire," the individual who actually created the work is its "author." In the case of a work made for hire, the statute provides that "the employer or other person for whom the work was prepared is considered the author."
- **What is a "Work Made for Hire"?** A "work made for hire" is defined as (1) "a work prepared by an employee within the scope of his or her employment"; or (2) "a work specially ordered or commissioned" for certain uses specified in the statute, but only if there is a written agreement to consider it a "work made for hire."
- **Collective Work:** In the case of a collective work, such as a song book or a collection of plays, it is sufficient to give information about the author of the collective work as a whole.
- **Author's Identity Not Revealed:** If an author's contribution is "anonymous" or "pseudonymous," it is not necessary to give the name and dates for that author. However, the citizenship or domicile of the author **must** be given in all cases, and information about the nature of that author's contribution to the work should be included.
- **Name of Author:** The fullest form of the author's name should be given. If you have checked "Yes" to indicate that the work was "made for hire," give the

full legal name of the employer (or other person for whom the work was prepared). You may also include the name of the employee (for example: "Music Makers Publishing Co. employer for hire of Lila Crane"). If the work is "anonymous" you may: (1) leave the line blank, or (2) state "Anonymous" in the line, or (3) reveal the author's identity. If the work is "pseudonymous" you may (1) leave the line blank, or (2) give the pseudonym and identify it as such (for example: "Huntley Haverstock, pseudonym"), or (3) reveal the author's name, making clear which is the real name and which is the pseudonym (for example: "Judith Barton, whose pseudonym is Madeleine Elster").

- **Dates of Birth and Death:** If the author is dead, the statute requires that the year of death be included in the application unless the work is anonymous or pseudonymous. The author's birth date is optional, but is useful as a form of identification. Leave this space blank if the author's contribution was a "work made for hire."
- **"Anonymous" or "Pseudonymous" Work:** An author's contribution to a work is "anonymous" if that author is not identified on the copies or phonorecords of the work. An author's contribution to a work is "pseudonymous" if that author is identified on the copies or phonorecords under a fictitious name.
- **Author's Nationality or Domicile:** Give the country of which the author is a citizen, or the country in which the author is domiciled. The statute requires that either nationality or domicile be given in all cases.
- **Nature of Authorship:** After the words "Author of" give a brief general statement of the nature of this particular author's contribution to the work. Examples: "Words"; "Co-Author of Music"; "Words and Music"; "Arrangement"; "Co-Author of Book and Lyrics"; "Dramatization"; "Entire Work"; "Compilation and English Translation"; "Editorial Revisions".

SPACE 3: CREATION AND PUBLICATION

- **General Instructions:** Do not confuse "creation" with "publication." Every application for copyright registration must state "the year in which creation of the work was completed." Give the date and nation of first publication only if the work has been published.
- **Creation:** Under the statute, a work is "created" when it is fixed in a copy or phonorecord for the first time. Where a work has been prepared over a period of time, the part of the work existing in fixed form on a particular date constitutes the created work on that date. The date you give here should be the year in which the author completed the particular version for which registration

is now being sought, even if other versions exist or if further changes or additions are planned.

- **Publication:** The statute defines "publication" as "the distribution of copies or phonorecords of a work to the public by sale or other transfer of ownership, or by rental, lease, or lending"; a work is also "published" if there has been an "offering to distribute copies or phonorecords to a group of persons for purposes of further distribution, public performance, or public display." Give the full date (month, day, year) when, and the country where, publication first occurred. If first publication took place simultaneously in the United States and other countries, it is sufficient to state "U.S.A."

SPACE 4: CLAIMANT(S)

- **Name(s) and Address(es) of Copyright Claimant(s):** Give the name(s) and address(es) of the copyright claimant(s) in this work. The statute provides that copyright in a work belongs initially to the author of the work (including, in the case of a work made for hire, the employer or other person for whom the work was prepared). The copyright claimant is either the author of the work or a person or organization that has obtained ownership of the copyright initially belonging to the author.

- **Transfer:** The statute provides that, if the copyright claimant is not the author, the application for registration must contain "a brief statement of how the claimant obtained ownership of the copyright." If any copyright claimant named in space 4 is not an author named in space 2, give a brief, general statement summarizing the means by which that claimant obtained ownership of the copyright.

CHAPTER 14

Writing Funny Songs

Through the ages, man has made fun of music, songwriters, musicians, and performers. I still hear trite lines like, "I can't even play my radio." Or, "I can't play anything but a radio, and all I get is static." Or, "Sing, 'Standing by the Window' and I'll help you out." Or "Sing that great old song, 'I Would Wear a Girdle But I Ain't Got the Guts.'"

I remember one spring when I was rehearsing a new road show and wanted to try it out on a live audience before taking it out for hire. I asked a friend of mine who owned a little beer joint if the band and I could set up and play for his customers just to get the feel of what we were doing. He agreed, so we hauled in all of our equipment, set up our show, and performed for one whole evening. Along about eleven P.M., a traveling salesman who had happened into the place sat and listened for a long time before staggering to his feet and yelling, "Hey, does Tom T. Hall know you're singing all his songs?"

There are a lot of funny songs written and a lot of good stories about songwriters. Some of them are too colorful to print here.

One of my favorite songwriting stories is about a man who came to Nashville and wanted to be a songwriter. A publisher liked his ideas, put him on a draw (advance against royalties), and gave him small room in which to write. The room had a tape recorder, typewriter, piano, guitar, and a bed. Two weeks later the publisher stopped by to see what the man had written. The songwriter said, "I haven't written anything in this crummy place you put me in. It's uncomfortable, and it's lonely, and that ain't all. The roof leaks."

The publisher said, "Well, this is all I can afford to offer you."

The songwriter said, "How do you expect me to write songs while 'Raindrops Keep Falling On My Head?'"

If you have a good sense of humor and like to write funny songs, I would advise you to go to it. Goodness knows we need them. I even like parodies of serious songs, but it's kind of a dangerous business if you don't get the original writer's permission. I know one fellow in Nashville who would beat you up for changing one of his songs around to sound funny.

Humorous songs are written by the same method I have encouraged you to use on other songs. However, I would caution you against trying to make a song of a joke. Once a joke has been told it seems to lose some of its punch. Maybe that's why they call the end of a joke a punch line.

If you want to write funny songs, you should try to find a humorous situation and not rely on one line to hold the entire song together.

Historically, songs of a funny nature have not fared as well as more serious ones. Humor can be a faddish thing that comes and goes according to the mood of the public, like the trends in clothing, music, lifestyle, and the political climate.

Over the years I have had a lot of fun writing songs for my friends on their birthdays or other occasions. I seldom publish these songs, but they please and entertain friends and it is good exercise in songwriting.

Roger Miller has written some of the cleverest songs we have had in Nashville in many a year; they were also big commercial successes.

I was once singing a new humorous song to a television producer. The director of the show said, "Louder!"

The producer of the show chimed in, "And funnier!"

CHAPTER 15

Dealing with Publishers

N ow you have the lyrics neatly typed and your song is on tape. Let's talk about how your effort gets to a publisher and what happens after it gets there.

The "Front Desk"

Let's walk into a publisher's office in Nashville. There's a young lady at the desk, and we'll ask her if there is anyone who will listen to some songs.

A publisher is usually a very busy individual, but I have found that if a person appears intelligent and appears to know where he is and what he's doing, a lot of publishers will have someone—maybe not the entire organization, but someone—who can listen to tapes. After all, they're in the songwriting and publishing business. You'll probably get turned down at a lot of places that won't listen to your tapes; but on occasion they will listen, and it won't take them very long to make an evaluation of your material. Nevertheless, being there and doing your best for your songs is what you want to do.

You've asked the lady if someone will listen to your songs, and she says, "Yes, we'll listen to your songs."

Your Song Is Heard

You go back to the little room where the fellow does all the listening. You sit down, and he sits down and puts your tape on a tape player. And he takes the lyrics and asks you about yourself and where you're from, and then he plays your tape. If he hears something in there he likes, he will say, "I like that very much and I'd like to keep it."

Then he may give you a standard songwriter's contract. I have included one for you on pages 92 and 93. It's the same kind I have used all these years, the kind my publisher has me sign. With this contract the publisher will get one-half the money your song makes because he is the publisher. You, the writer, get the other 50 percent. He does everything that has to be done to that song. He'll have it copyrighted, he'll have it published, he'll do his best to have it recorded, and he'll do his best to see that you get as much money out of it as he does.

Being a songwriter and being a publisher are absolutely two different things; that's why I think it's important for you to take your tape and song to someone in whom you have confidence. You don't want to have to worry about publishing.

The Song Is Placed

As we progress, I would like to congratulate you on making contact with a publisher and getting your song placed.

Now the term *placed* means simply that you have gotten the song accepted by either a publisher or an artist. You have put it in a place where it has a chance to become something.

What does a publisher do with that song?

First of all, he publishes it. Unfortunately, that doesn't make you any money. Some people say, "Well, he had a song published; he should be getting money." But the only way you can make money from a song is to have it sell, and that's something else. That means having it actually on the market where it's being performed or selling records or albums.

We'll talk about that in a little bit.

Getting a Lead Sheet

A publisher will have a lead sheet made. He'll hand your tape and lyrics to someone in the building who will go off and make up the sheet music for the company files and for the copyright office.

The copyright of the song will be in your name as writer and in the name of the publisher.

It's the publisher who worries about these things. You need have no concern now. Because you have your signed copy of the songwriter's contract, you're protected.

What Next?

A publisher cannot make money with a song unless he gets someone else interested in it, so he goes to all the record companies, movie people, Broadway people, and anyone else who uses music. He is the distributor of that music.

That gives you more time to write.

The Demo Session

The publisher may want to make a demonstration record. This is no expense for you. Because the publisher receives 50 percent of what this song makes, he assumes the responsibility to make the song a success. So he takes the song to a studio, hires a group of musicians, and has a demo session. The recording is not for sale; it's merely to demonstrate the song to people who might be interested in it.

Your song may be on a session with several other songs he has, maybe from other writers. Maybe he'll take two or three of your songs along if he likes your writing well enough. After making the demo, he will turn it over to a man at the publishing company who "pitches" it.

Pitching the Song

Pitching a song is like making a sales pitch for any product. The man who pitches songs (often called a "song plugger") goes to an artist or his producer or A & R (artist and repertory) man, the one who handles the arrangements and everything for the artist. He says, "I really think this is a good song." So he makes a sales pitch.

Now if the A & R man—the producer—likes the song and the artist likes the song, then they are going to make a record of it for

STANDARD SONGWRITERS CONTRACT

Agreement made this _____ day of _____, 19___, between

HALLNOTE MUSIC COMPANY in Brentwood, Tennessee (hereinafter called the "Publisher") and

Witnesseth:

In consideration of the agreement herein contained and of the sum of One (1.00) Dollar and other good and valuable consideration in hand paid by the Publisher to the Writer (s), receipt of which is hereby acknowledged, the parties agree as follows:

1. The Writer (s) hereby sells, assigns, transfers and delivers to the Publisher, its successors and assigns, a certain heretofore unpublished original musical composition, written and/or composed by the above named writer (s), now entitled:

including the title, words and music, and all copyrights thereof, including but not limited to the copyright registration thereof No. _____, and all rights, claims and demands in any way relating thereto, and the exclusive right to secure copyright therein throughout the entire world, and to have and to hold the said copyrights and all rights of whatsoever nature now and hereafter thereunder existing and/or existing under any agreements of licenses relating thereto, for and during the full terms of all of said copyrights. In consideration of the agreement to pay royalties herein contained and other good and valuable consideration in hand paid by the Publisher to the Writer (s), receipt of which is hereby acknowledged, the Writer (s) hereby sells, assigns, transfers and delivers to the Publisher, its successors and assigns, all renewal and extentions of the copyrights of said musical compositions (s) to which the Writer (s) may be entitled hereafter, and all registrations thereof, and all rights of any and every nature now and hereafter thereunder existing, for the full terms of all such renewals and extensions of copyrights.

2. The Writer(s) hereby warrants that the said composition is his sole, exclusive and original work, and that he has full right and power to make the within agreement, and that there exists no adverse claims to or in the said composition. The Writer (s) hereby further warrants and represents that he is not a member of the American Society of Composers, Authors and Publishers, the Songwriters' Protective Association, or of any other society or association which requires as a condition of membership the assignment of any right of any kind in said musical work and that no assignment of any of the rights herein set forth has been directly or indirectly made to Broadcast Music, Inc. or any other person, firm or corporation whatsoever.

3. The Writer (s) hereby warrant(s) that the foregoing musical composition is new and original and does not infringe any other copyrighted work and has been created by the joint collaboration of the Writers named herein and that said composition, including the title, words and music thereof, has been, unless herein otherwise specifically noted, the result of the joint efforts of all the undersigned Writers and not by way of any independent or separable activity by any of the Writers.

4. In consideration of this agreement, the Publisher agrees to pay the Writer (s) during the original and renewal terms of copyright throughout the world as follows:

(a) In respect of regular piano copies sold and paid for at wholesale in the United States of America, royalties of three cents per copy;

(b) A royalty of five cents per copy of dance orchestrations thereof sold and paid for in the United States of America;

(c) A royalty of ten per cent of all net earned sums received by the Publisher in respect of regular piano copies and/or orchestrations thereof sold and paid for in any foreign country by a foreign publisher.

(d) The sum equal to ten percent of any moneys received by publisher when the said composition is published in any folio or composite work or lyric magazine by the Publisher or licensees of the Publisher. Such publication may be made at any time in the discretion of the Publisher;

(e) In respect of copies sold and rights licensed or sold in the Dominion of Canada, the royalties to be paid to the Writer (s) shall be on the same royalty basis as herein provided for sales or licenses in the United States.

(f) As to "professional material"— Not sold or resold, no royalty shall be payable;

(g) An amount equal to fifty per cent of all net earned proceeds received and actually retained by the Publisher arising out of (1) the manufacture of phonograph records and other parts of instruments serving to mechanically reproduce said composition, or (2) the use of said composition in synchronization with sound motion pictures;

(h) Except as herein expressly provided, no other royalties shall be paid with respect to the said composition.

(i) Notwithstanding anything contained in this agreement, the Publisher shall deduct ten percent of all net receipts from all licenses issued by it to licensees in the United States and elsewhere, as collection charges for the collection of the proceeds of such licenses, before computing the royalties payable under paragraph 4 of this agreement.

5. The Publisher shall render the Writers, as above, on or before each August 15th covering the six months ending June 30th; and each February 15th covering the six months ending December 31st, royalty statements accompanied by remittance for any royalties due thereunder.

6. Anything to the contrary notwithstanding, nothing in this agreement contained shall obligate the Publisher to print copies of said composition or shall prevent the Publisher from authorizing publishers, agents and representatives in countries inside and outside of the United States from exercising exclusive publication and all other rights in said foreign countries in said composition on the customary royalty basis, it being understood that the percentage of the Writer(s) on moneys received from foreign sources shall be computed on the Publisher(s) net receipts; and nothing in this agreement shall prevent the Publisher from authorizing publishers in the United States from exercising exclusive publication rights and other rights in the United States in said composition, provided the Publisher shall pay the Writer(s) the royalties herein stipulated.

7. The Writer(s) may appoint a certified public accountant who shall, upon written request therefore, have access to all records of the Publisher during business hours relating to said composition for the purpose of verifying royalty statements hereunder.

8. The Writer(s) hereby consent to such changes, adaptations, dramatizations, transpositions, editing and arrangements of said composition, and the setting of words to the music and of music to the words, and the change of title as the Publisher deems desirable. The Writer(s) hereby waive any and all claims which they have or may have against the Publisher and/or its associated, affiliated and subsidiary corporations by reason of the fact the title of said composition may be the same or similar to that of any musical composition or compositions heretofore or hereafter acquire by the Publisher and/or its associated, affiliated and subsidiary corporations. The Writer(s) consents to the use of his (their) name and likeness and the title to the said composition on the music, folios, recordings, performances, player rolls and in connection with publicity and advertising concerning the Publisher, its successors, assigns and licensees, and said composition, and agrees that the use of such name, likeness and title may commence prior to publication and may continue so long as the Publisher shall own and/or exercise any rights in said composition.

9. Written demands and notices other than royalty statements provided for herein shall be sent by registered mail.

10. Any legal action brought by the Publisher against any alleged infringer of said composition shall be initiated and prosecuted at the Publisher's sole expense, and of any recovery made by it as a result thereof, after deduction of the expense of the litigation, a sum equal to thirty-three and one-third (33-1/3) per cent shall be paid to the Writer(s).

(a) If a claim is presented against the Publisher in respect of said composition, and because thereof the Publisher is jeopardized, it shall thereupon serve written notice upon the Writer(s), containing the full details of such claim known to the Publisher and thereafter until the claim has been adjudicated or settled shall hold any moneys coming due the Writer(s) in escrow pending the outcome of such claim or claims. The Publisher shall have the right to settle or otherwise dispose of such claims in any manner as it in its sole discretion may determine. In the event of any recovery against the Publisher, either by way of judgment or settlement, all of the costs, charges, disbursements, attorney fees and the amount of the judgment or settlement, may be deducted by the Publisher from any and all royalties or other payments therefore or thereafter payable to the Writer(s) by the Publisher or by its associated, affiliated, or subsidiary corporations.

(b) From and after the service of summons in a suit for infringement filed against the Publisher with respect to said composition, any and all payments thereafter coming due the Writer(s) shall be held by the Publisher in trust until the suit has been adjudicated and then be disbursed accordingly, unless the Writer(s) shall elect to file an acceptable bond in the sum of payments, in which event the sums due shall be paid to the Writer(s).

11. "Writer" as used herein shall be deemed to include all authors and composers signing this agreement.

12. The Writer(s), each for himself, hereby irrevocably constitute and appoint the Publisher or any of its officers, directors, or general manager, his (their) attorney and representative, in the name(s) of the Writer(s), or any of them, or in the name of the Publisher, its successors and assigns, to make, sign, execute, acknowledge and deliver any and all instruments which may be desirable or necessary in order to vest in the Publisher, its successors and assigns, any of the rights hereinabove referred to.

13. The Publisher shall have the right to sell, assign, transfer, license or otherwise dispose of any of its rights in whole or in part under this agreement to any person, firm or corporation, but said disposition shall not affect the right of the Writer(s) to the royalties hereinabove set forth.

14. This agreement shall be binding upon and shall inure to the benefit of the respective parties hereto, their respective successors in interest, legal representatives and assigns, and represents the entire understanding between the parties.

15. Notwithstanding anything contained in this agreement, the Publisher shall not be held responsible for collection of any royalties due Writer(s) for broadcast performance fees earned by the aforementioned composition. Performance fees due Writer(s) shall be paid directly by Broadcast Music, Inc. who is the publishers licensing Agent, for performances. Application for collection of such royalties should be made by Writer(s) directly to Broadcast Music, Inc. upon the recorded release of composition.

IN WITNESS WHEREOF, the parties hereto have hereunto set their hands and seals the day and year first above written.

By_____

Writer_____

Address_____

Writer_____

Address_____

Writer_____

Address_____

you. If not, the publisher will bring the song back to the office and try to pitch it to someone else.

It's rare for a publisher to try to pitch a song to the same person twice. It's also rare for a publisher to give a song back to a writer if he doesn't do anything with it; a lot of songs have lain around for five or six or seven years.

You have to understand that the publisher has his money invested in the lead sheets and demo sessions, and it's a considerable amount of money. Only if he holds onto the song can he hope to make that money back. "You Gave Me a Mountain" and "There Goes My Everything" are only two of the many successful songs that were hits a number of years after they were actually written.

I wouldn't be concerned about my song not being returned. If you hadn't wanted to make the deal, and you hadn't wanted to make the publisher responsible for that song, you shouldn't have placed it there in the first place. He is going to play it for everyone who will listen to it; it is his business to get songs recorded, into movie soundtracks, anywhere he can make money with the song.

Keep the Faith

If you write a couple of songs and the publisher can't do anything with them, even though he likes them, don't give up on him. You have found a man who likes your music. Instead of complaining, the thing to do is to keep taking new material back to him. If he's really interested in your material and your songs are good, eventually he will get one cut.

If he gets one recorded, he probably can get some of the others recorded, too. Once you've had a song recorded and it has been a hit, he can say, "Well, how would you like to hear some more of this man's material? I have some more here that he wrote earlier. We haven't had any reaction to them yet."

Keep Writing

Keep on writing. Don't be like some people I have met who brought me songs in 1969 and three years later were back in Nashville with the same songs. They hadn't written another line or another word. They were still trying to get those same songs recorded.

Unfortunately, songwriting is not a business of one hit or two or three hits. It's a life-long occupation and profession. To really make a good living at it (and to enjoy it), you have to write all the time. So if those first songs don't make it, put them on the shelf and write some more; that's what songwriting is all about. It's just like every other job. You can't work three days as president of the United States and quit; you have to put in four years.

Now I would like to congratulate you again. You've had your song recorded. Remember, you went to see the publisher, he liked your song, he had a demo tape made, he played it for an artist and producer, and they recorded it. The first thing you'll probably do is lie awake all night listening for someone to play your record on the radio. I hope you hear it.

I'm sure you will.

CHAPTER 16

How You Get Paid?

How are you going to make any money? This is very difficult to explain; but at the same time it is very simple. This is not legal talk, and I don't want you to hand this to a lawyer to see what he thinks about it, because I'm not a lawyer. I am a songwriter, and I am telling you the way I see it.

The details may differ on occasion; but, generally speaking, when you have a song recorded, the publisher will receive four cents for every record sold. If two of your songs are on the record, the publisher will get eight cents for every record sold. You and the publisher will split that money fifty-fifty, two cents for you for each one of your songs on a record that's sold, and two cents for the publisher.

Getting an Accounting

In your songwriter's contract you will note that the publisher is obligated to pay you twice a year. He will give you an accounting every six months.

Performance Fees

Performance rights provide another source of income. I know of three performance rights societies that license music for performance.

They are BMI (Broadcast Music Incorporated, with which I am associated), ASCAP, and SESAC. ASCAP is the American Society of

Composers, Authors, and Publishers. SESAC's name comes from the organization's formative days when it was active only in Europe. Today the initials just stand for "SESAC."

Each time your record is played on the radio, you supposedly receive about two and one-half cents. This differs with the various licensing agencies. They have different plans if you stay with them a long time and if your songs play a lot. But basically you can consider that you will receive two and one-half cents for each time one of your songs is played on the radio.

You don't need to keep track of that yourself; in fact, you can't do it. If you live in Boston, you're not going to know if they play your record in Tuscaloosa. So a licensing agency like BMI, ASCAP, or SESAC, with which the publisher will affiliate you, takes care of all that.

If a publisher wants to publish your song, he will tell you how to go about joining one of the performance rights societies. The publishing companies are affiliated with these agencies for performances, and you have to belong to the one with which your publisher is affiliated.

We call the performance money just that—performance money. Here is the way it's normally paid. On occasion (which, by the way, is the secret of the licensing organization) they keep a log of all the tunes the radio stations play during a certain period of time. They take this log, which they get from making spot checks around the country, and figure an average for all of the radio stations that play that kind of music. More or less, they take a poll of what's playing at that time, and you are paid according to the poll.

There's no way anyone could know every time a song is played on the radio, but it's as fair for one writer as it is for another. The licensing agencies give to the songwriters the money they collect, keeping, I believe, only a small percentage for operations.

I am explaining this to you in lay terms because I am not a performance rights expert. But I want to tell you what I know about it in words that are simple and accurate. If you want greater detail than this, you will need to talk to an expert in performance rights.

Mechanicals

Performance money is just called "performance money." Record sales, on the other hand, are called "mechanicals." This goes back to the days of player-piano rolls. It was a mechanical process—the moving piano roll had holes in it—and so the copyright law was written as a mechanical, but we still call record sales "mechanicals."

If a publisher tells you that you have a certain amount coming in mechanicals, he means record sales; and he'll pay you for that. You normally get your performance money direct from the licensing agency (BMI, ASCAP, or SESAC), and you get your mechanicals from the publisher.

Under some circumstances the writer will make a deal with the publisher to collect his performance royalties also. I do not recommend that the writer make any such deal.

Live and Television Performances

Royalties for live performances are probably the most difficult for the performance rights societies to collect. If someone in a cocktail lounge sings one of your songs, it is hard for the society to know this. Many of the small clubs do not secure a license to perform any one society's songs. Since such clubs and places of entertainment are so numerous, it is almost impossible for anyone to police them in order to log performances. The financial cost of enforcing compliance would be far more than the society would collect from these clubs, lounges, bars, and theaters.

On larger concert dates, where the money is considerable and better track can be kept of the performances, money is collected and distributed to the writers in the same fashion as the money due from radio and TV exposure.

On TV performances, the money is collected in much the same manner as for radio performances, except that different fees are set for prime time, network, and reruns.

I think it is fair to say that the performance societies are as interested in collecting monies due a writer as the writer is. A writer wants to be assured that all of his performance money is being collected. From the time I became a BMI writer, I have not had the slightest doubt that the organization was doing everything possible to get me as much money as it could from people who use my music for public, broadcast, or telecast purposes.

Videos

If a record company wants to do a video of one of your songs, it will probably be considered recorded promotion and you will be paid the same as if someone had performed your song on any other show.

If they make a movie or a commercial of your song, or use your song in one, you have what is called "Grand Rights." That means that they can't use your idea without paying. The price they pay is negotiable, and your publisher will negotiate for you. He'll probably ask for Texas and settle for Dallas.

CHAPTER 17

A Few More Do's and Don'ts

In this chapter I want to offer a few words of caution about attitudes and your feelings about yourself. You will do well if you keep these matters in mind.

Be Yourself

I want to warn you about a subtle danger you face in trying hard to become a songwriter. In all the things you do, like staying alert to song possibilities, making notes, finding a place to write, and setting aside time for writing, you face a danger. Even if you have the place and the time, have learned the rules and mastered the rest, you can't sit down to write as a writer. Sit down as a person.

When you're overly aware of being a writer, it can be a great handicap. Songs aren't written by songwriters; they're written by people. My most difficult task when sitting down to write is to remember that I am just a person who has something to say. If I suddenly become poetic, dramatic, or phony, it hurts my writing. I can't say, "The night was as black as the eyes of sin, and the moon looked like a huge hole in the sky." That is not the way I think.

If you are a tyro, you may be tempted to write the way you know others do, but that is the way they express *their* thoughts. If you imitate someone else, you are being dishonest with your thoughts. Always remember to say it as you see it. If you want to write a song about a man who stole a bunch of grapes, where do you start? Well, how about a line like this: "I knew a man who stole a bunch of grapes!"

Hell, yes! That's not a bad idea!

101

It's All Been Said

On my first day in Music City, U.S.A., someone told me, "Tom T., it's all been said. You just have to express the same thing in a different light."

I was all set to write about things no one had written about before. Love, hate, fear, hunger—none of these were for me; my aim was to shake the world. But it took only a few days of strumming my guitar and pounding on my typewriter to realize that love, hate, fear, loneliness, and happiness were the main ingredients in any song.

One night, on one of my first visits backstage at the world-famed Grand Ole Opry, Bill Anderson, a great songwriter, introduced himself and said he liked my songs. I was a little embarrassed and replied that I was just writing what people had already written in one way or another. Bill studied his boots for a minute, looked at me, and said, "Yeah, I guess that's what we're all doing."

Bitterness Is Bad

Bitterness is bad company. If you let yourself get carried away with notions that "they've got it in for me" or "ole so-and-so doesn't like me and all the other producers don't want to do anything that would make him mad" or any other self-pitying foolishness, you can forget about having success in the music business. Creative people busy trying to make music are uncomfortable around a person who harps on the evils of those who fail to become part of his own scheme for wealth and glory. A good friend doesn't mind giving you the opportunity to let off steam occasionally, but it is foolish to let your complaints begin to sound like the proverbial broken record.

We Have Met the Enemy

It has often been said that the music business is a clique, that it's a small group of people banded together to put out contracts on struggling songwriters, to have them murdered in their sleep—in short, to do everything they can to keep the beginners from making any progress. It seems as if every time someone has a song turned down he says, "I was turned down in Nashville" or "I was out in Los Angeles (or Chicago or New York) and they didn't like my material."

"They didn't like my material?" Who are *they?*

The most interesting thing about the music business is that it is made up of people who love the same thing and who are in fierce competition with each other. I'm in competition with every other writer; that's what I do for a living. If he writes better than I do, then he gets to pay the rent and put the butter on the bread and I don't. Nashville, Los Angeles, New York, and Chicago are full of music people. The world is full of music people; the people of the world love music. But they're all in competition with each other, and to band them all together for anything other than a beer party is almost impossible.

In fact, if there's a young writer in town and someone thinks he has some pretty good songs, every publisher in town wants to hear a few of his tunes. They want to see the man. They want to talk to him. The music business is a business, and publishers, record producers, and artists are looking for songs. Songs are the things that make the music business what it is. They are our raw material, much as pulpwood is to the paper industry or iron ore is to the steel industry. Your success will depend on your songs, because, as far as I'm concerned, songs are where it's at.

So until you have played that song for every artist, musician, entertainer, publisher, record producer, and music fan in the world, you can't legitimately say "they" are against you or don't like your song. You may be frustrated and discouraged, and you may think people really are banded together to keep new writers out of town.

But that's really sort of silly. It's like assuming that because oil was struck in Texas the oil industry of the world wouldn't be interested if you had oil in your backyard. They'd be there digging tomorrow. Publishers are the same way. It's a very competitive business. If you've got musical gold in your soul, publishers are looking for you.

At the writing cabin retreat.

If you decide you want to make your living as a songwriter and decide that Nashville is the best setting for your particular personality and talent (and that should be your *primary* reason for moving here), I assure you that you will find plenty to complain about, just as you would if you moved to New York and Los Angeles.

But be careful. Being known as somebody who works harder at bitching than at writing can have a negative effect on your acceptance as a writer.

No Open Sesames

Something else: I once heard WSM Radio personality Hairl Hensley read a letter on the air from a listener somewhere in the Midwest. The writer used the phrase "I sure want to be a star" two or three times, and he seemed to think that a simple telephone call to Porter Waggoner would assure him of that status. Therefore, he was asking Hairl for help in getting Porter's telephone number. You've heard that old expression, "It's not what you know—it's who you know," applies more to the entertainment business than it does to anything else, but don't you believe it. Knowing Porter Wag-goner or Johnny Cash or Tom T. Hall, for that matter, won't help if you can't deliver the goods.

I have a lot of friends who have not "made it," and most of them have tried very diligently. I have been able to help most of them in some, usually indirect, ways. Most often I was able to make people who had a need for their talents aware of their abilities. But being a friend of mine has not opened up any doors for them. The record-buying public is the only final authority we have in the music busi-ness. Unless you have the blessings of that public, which buys your records and goes to your shows, it doesn't really matter who you know.

So what is Nashville? A good town. An interesting city popu-lated by half a million average American citizens and several hun-dred of the world's most creative minds. Waylon Jennings told a New York night club audience, "I hope you all like what we do. If you don't—don't ever come to Nashville. We'll kick the hell out of you." The reality isn't quite that colorful, but as a beginning song-writer I think it would be important for you to like what we do in Nashville before you come here to be a part of it. Adjustment prob-lems can make you feel as if we were indeed kicking the hell out of you.

If you move to Nashville and constantly complain that "nobody in Nashville knows what to do" with a favorite song you have writ-ten and "it's gonna take somebody on the West Coast to do it," then you should be on the West Coast showing your song to people out there. I have a friend who has appeared in three major motion pictures, and the closest he's ever been to Hollywood is Los Angeles International Airport for two hours on a layover between Sacra-mento and Nashville. He didn't have to move to Hollywood to get in the movies, and you don't have to move to Nashville to write songs. I live in Nashville because I like it and because some people here were interested in my music and gave me an outlet for my writing. If that outlet had turned out to be New York or Rome or Rio, my situation today would probably be different. But I like writing songs, and that's what's important.

Live wherever you are comfortable and wherever you have access to people who could possibly have a need for your music. A center of concentrated activity in the music business is helpful, but don't get the idea that just living in Nashville is going to make you a writer. It won't.

Don't Sell Your Songs

Although many song contracts make a reference to selling your songs, I would like to point out that the word *sell* does not apply in the same sense it does when you sell a house or a car. In most songwriter contracts you will note that a great deal of control over the song is given back to the writer in one paragraph or another. The word *sell* is used simply to protect the publisher in his considerable responsibility to you as a writer. Do not think that you are literally selling your song for "one dollar and other valuable considerations," as most contracts will read. The contract must be regarded in its entirety.

Here is a little story I think might discourage you from selling any of your songs for a sum of money and not retaining any of the rights granted a composer in a standard contract. A certain young man from the Midwest came into a large recording center to pick up a few bucks with his songs without going through the normal processes of waiting for a recording, sales, performance, or any other action to take place. Driving into town and stopping at the first music business office he came to, he offered to sell his songs outright for fifty dollars each. The people he first talked to were not interested in buying his songs and didn't really care much about them.

Not discouraged by his first failure to sell his songs, he looked around for other buyers. His next meeting was at a night spot where a lot of recording artists went to relax. Although he was still trying to sell his songs to someone, he had a very fortunate break. The next man he encountered was a popular recording artist who knew the young man was making a mistake. The artist told the young man he would record his songs, but the young man would receive proper royalties for them.

The songs were recorded, and the young man is now a successful songwriter. The point of this story is that a writer should not be too impatient with the mechanics of the business. Another very important point is that you do not have to sell your songs in order to get them recorded. The young man who tried to sell his songs thought that artists or publishers would be interested in his songs only if they could own them and put their names on them. In his rush to get a song published and recorded, he was willing to give up his authorship and ownership of them, thinking that this would entice people to be more interested.

I have had people offer me half or all of a song if I would record it. My standard reply is that I make enough money when I record a hit song and I consider a song only on its merits. Ownership has nothing to do with my selection of material. There have been times in the music business when recording personalities have asked for part ownership of a song before he or she would record it. Maybe this is still being done; if so, that is probably where this young man got the impression that that's the way the business works.

If an artist thinks a song will be a hit, he will want it regardless of who owns it. My answer to anyone who wants part of one of my songs in order to record it is a flat, unqualified no! I have always detested anyone who would ask for a part of something he or she did not create, and I would recommend that you tell anyone who asks you for this kind of deal to go to hell, as bluntly or as subtly as you will.

You must understand—especially when you're starting out—that one man's opinion is not the death of a song. I have on occasion been criticized for something I have written. Someone called it a piece of crap. Later that same song was recorded and became very successful, and I made a good bit of money. So if the first person you encounter—the first publisher or the first producer, record company representative or whoever—turns down your song, do not be disappointed or discouraged.

Food for thought.

Song Blindness

I talked earlier about songs being children. If you start off with an idea and it becomes a verse, then a bridge or a chorus, then another verse, and finally it becomes a song with a beginning, an end, a melody, a message, and a purpose, then that song is not unlike a child you have watched grow and become healthy and impressive.

For that reason, you have to be very careful. You cannot let yourself become so attached to a song that you forget to be critical of your own work.

The cattlemen who raise the purebred black Angus, the registered Charolais, the Herefords, and the many other fine breeds of cattle have an expression: barn blindness. It applies to a man who has raised a herd of cattle, who has watched them grow from the time they were little calves, who knows their sire and their dam, and who thinks his calves are the best cattle on any ranch in the world. Because he's near them, he knows all their personality quirks. He's able to appreciate them for many more reasons than the average cattle buyer would. The buyer sees only that it's black, has four legs, a head, and tail; it's a cow, and that's about the extent of it as far as he's concerned. He didn't sit up all night nursing it on a bottle, and he didn't watch it grow and frolic about the pasture.

So it is with our songs. Although they may be great and very dear to us, let's not have "song blindness."

Look at your songs openly and honestly. The most difficult thing in the world for a writer to do is to be critical of his own songs, his own material. On occasion you will find your song just "needs something," but you can't put your finger on it. There is something about it you don't like. You know it's not quite finished, you know it doesn't quite say what you want it to say, you know the melody isn't just right. Yet you're a little tired of the idea you have for this song, and so you wrap it up. Then you put it on a tape and try to sneak it by someone. You play it for them and hope they won't notice the short-change in the song. You hope they won't hear the poorly related lyrics and the not-too-well-associated melody.

On occasion you will find a sympathetic ear, someone who is impressed with the fact that you are a songwriter. You can sing them what obviously is not a very good song, and they might say, "That's pretty good." Well, if we could make a career out of writing pretty good songs, there would be a lot more people in the business than there are.

"Spooks"

The term *spook* refers to a person who keeps bothering someone in the music business with his ideas, songs, music, adoration—without regard for that person's privacy, schedule, or time.

You want to avoid the possibility of becoming a spook or a bug. A case in point is this: A man and his wife—with three kids trailing along—drove up to my private residence in an automobile, parked the car, came up and banged on the door, and wanted to get me to listen to some of their songs. They had a huge suitcase full of tapes and lyrics, and they were very enthusiastic. The man kept telling me what a great opportunity this would be for me to become rich and famous, to record all of his songs and show them to other prominent people in the music business. Had he been Cole Porter, Kris Kristofferson, or Burt Bacharach, that man could not have gotten even one of his songs in consideration at my home that morning.

People in the music business who publish and record songs and who write professionally have great respect for the time and the manner in which they present their material.

If you want to place your material, you must realize that publishers and artists and people of prominence in the music business are continuously bombarded with requests to listen to someone's material and/or performance. So when you make your presentation, be sure it is at the proper time—during office hours—at the proper place—in their office. If you have an appointment, present yourself on time and as courteously as you can. Take into consideration that you are among the many. Be sure your lyrics and tapes are in order and that you are neat, well-dressed, and well-mannered. This way you will have a much better chance of getting a reputable publisher to take a look at your songs and give you consideration.

Vanity Records

When you have tried every source you know to get your song recorded, to no avail, what do you do then?

If you think you have a good song, I know you are dying to get it recorded. I have heard it said a million times, "If I could just hear one of my songs on the radio one time, I'd be the happiest person in the world." That, of course, is not true. When you hear one of your records on the radio one time, you'll be mad as hell if you don't hear it twice. If you hear it seven or eight times, you'll be mad as hell if it doesn't become a big hit. If it does become a big hit, you'll be frantic if you can't get another.

One of the wisest statements I have ever heard about success was made by a bookkeeper friend of mine: "Enough is a bit more."

If you are going to spend money to record your song, have three hundred records made, pass them around among your friends, and take one to the local disc jockey and ask him to give you some advice. But don't expect much to happen.

There are ways by which you can do exactly what I have outlined. You can take your songs to any of the major recording centers, such as Nashville, New York, Chicago, Memphis, or Los Angeles, and make three hundred copies of a record, with a vocalist (yourself, if you like), a band, and sound effects. This will cost you from a thousand to fifteen hundred dollars, depending on the quality of the musicians and the operational methods of the firm with which you do business.

I do not recommend "vanity" publishing and recording. In almost every case you get only what you buy: three hundred records.

If you have fifteen hundred or two thousand dollars you would like to spend just to have a record with your name on it, go ahead and spend it. There is a chance the opportunities some of these firms offer you will happen. And thereby hangs the sales pitch. In fact, they can point you to an instance where all of what they offer has happened. However, you have equally as much chance of finding a wallet with several thousand dollars in it as you walk down the street.

Most of the people who make vanity records expound the laws of probability. What they talk about could happen—no one can say it cannot—and so their promises are legal. And they serve a certain portion of the writers who like to gamble. Your odds, however, could be a lot better at a crap table in Las Vegas.

CHAPTER 18

What Is Nashville?

Everybody knows what Nashville is. It's a city, the capital of Tennessee, home of the Grand Ole Opry, the "Nashville Sound," Chet Atkins, Minnie Pearl, "Hee-Haw," and The Nashville Network.

Nashville is the only city in the United States with the graves of two former U.S. presidents (Andrew Jackson and James K. Polk), and her overall contribution to our history is fitting of the honor.

But to you, an aspiring songwriter, Nashville is important for another set of reasons, reasons tied rather closely to the "Home of Country Music" image. Nashville is one of the world's primary work centers for the entertainment industry and a strategic center for country music.

That doesn't mean you have to live in Nashville to be active in country music. But if you attain a degree of success that enables you to earn a major portion of your livelihood from country music, it will be necessary for you at least to come in contact with people who do live here. It is impossible to ignore or avoid Nashville if you are to have success.

For that reason, it would be wise for you to familiarize yourself with Nashville's music community and all its assets, liabilities, possibilities, and improbabilities. Putting all of that in print would require another book, but I can offer a few suggestions that should aid you in making your own discoveries. That's the best way to learn. By learning for yourself, you become familiar with the aspects of Nashville that are important to you and your career. Those that are important to Tom. T. Hall may have an altogether different meaning for you.

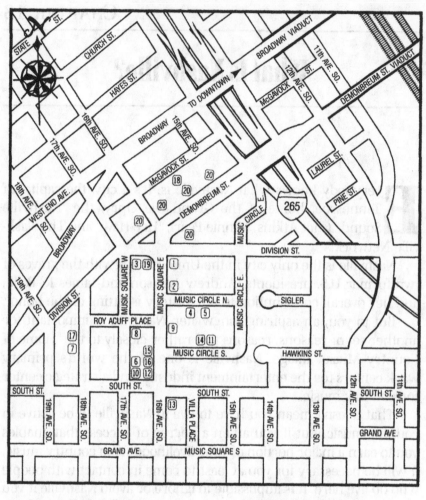

1. Country Music Hall of Fame
2. Broadcast Music Inc.
3. ASCAP
4. Nashville Association of Musicians
5. Country Music Association
6. Gospel Music Association
7. Nashville Songwriters Association
8. RCA
9. CBS
10. Warner Brothers
11. Polygram & Mercury
12. Stargem
13. Welk Music Group
14. Ronnie Milsap Enterprises
15. Combine Music Group
16. Denny Music Group
17. Porter Waggoner Enterprises
18. Jim Owens Entertainment
19. Music Square Park
20. Gift Shop Area

"Music Row" in Nashville, during the mid-eighties.

The Key Is Work

Remember that Nashville is a work center of the entertainment industry, much more than it is an entertainment center. If you want to smother yourself in glamour and glory, go to Las Vegas or Miami Beach. Or New York, Hollywood, or Disneyland.

Although there is a certain amount of glory surrounding the music business in Nashville, and the tour operators show you lavish houses, and a lot of expensive cars are parked on 16th and 17th avenues, nevertheless the key word in Nashville is *work*.

Some people relish the image of the songwriter who sits around a bar boozing it up with his buddies for days on end until suddenly an idea for the supersmash hit record of the century forms in his mind and he writes it down on a napkin. Enough of that happens to fertilize the seeds of fancy, but the reality is that songwriting is much like any other business. Before you can expect to buy the houses and cars, you have to write songs and get some of them recorded by people who can turn them into hits.

The way creativity works varies from person to person, but no law says you can't allot a certain amount of time each day to work at the craft of writing songs. A tool and die maker sets aside a certain amount of his time for his craft. In fact, it's a safe bet that applying basic good business principles to the business of writing songs will bring you a lot closer to the payoff.

Now I'm not saying that writing songs is no different from tool and die work. Writing songs is not the same as grinding out something you have a pattern for, with no inspirational creativity involved. It is different in many respects. I think that's why so many people are drawn to writing songs; it gives them a sense of satisfaction they've never been able to find doing anything else. But if you plan to make a living by songwriting, you have to remember it is a business.

Another matter: The people who turn down your song material are not necessarily your enemies. They are right sometimes, and they are wrong sometimes. But usually they try to make the right decisions.

Now You're Part of a Team

Recording is very personal. Just as a song proclaims a writer's private thinking to the public, a record has similar origins. The singer delivers the song in a manner that sells himself or herself as well as the song. For that reason, selecting material is a complicated personal matter that is done with more reliance upon instinct than on facts and figures. The musicians work to provide a vehicle for the singer and the song. Their skill comes from long practice and from years of "just gittin' in there and doin' it." The recording engineer's job is more technical, perhaps; but it, too, requires a lot of feeling—instinct, if you like. This instinct comes only from being experienced in recording. Finally the producer ties all of these efforts together, producing a true team enterprise.

That team must include a songwriter. Without the song there can be no record. But a lot of factors that may never come to full light affect whether or not you are chosen as the writer in a particular recording team.

So they're not lining you up before a firing squad when they turn down your songs; they're putting somebody else on their team for that game. The more you play, and the more impressive you become in practice (which is, in this instance, simply showing your songs), the more likely you are to be included the next time they record.

CHAPTER 19

Analyzing
Some of the Songs I've Written

S ince the beginning of the book I've been talking about what you should do and how you should do it. I have urged you to give free rein to your inspirations, observations, and creative urges. I've explained the creative process in general, at least Tom T. Hall's creative process. And I've summarized the music industry's daily business operations.

Now I would like to guide you through a brief analysis of some of the songs I've written. By explaining to you the germination of my ideas and how they later developed, I might be able to help you lock in on your own inspirations and encourage you to work on them until you've completed a song.

I'm providing leadsheets—sheet music—and the lyrics. In the first part of this section I'll assist in the analytical process. In the second section I'll let you do it yourself.

I've chosen these songs because they show a wide variety of approaches to subject matter and style. Also, I've made reference of some of these songs earlier in this book.

How I Wrote "I See"

This is the best example of my songwriting that I can offer. It was not a single record, so we'll never know if it could have been a big hit. But in this song I have used my method of songwriting to best advantage, and that's why I call it my best example.

I SEE

By TOM T. HALL

1. I see a boy and a girl ___ in a pick-up truck,

Snug-gled to-geth-er and so much in love,

Smiles on their fac-es, they sure look pleased, I see.

2. I
I see.

3. I
I see.

2. I see an old man cutting fire place wood,
Big red jacket and big red hood;
Here on the highway the smoke smells good,
I see.

3. I see a little dog on the side of the road,
Long been dead and long been cold.
I see a little boy about five years old,
I see.

4. I see a young man, his shoes full of holes,
Working in a car wash and his hands are cold,
And that was me some time ago,
I see.

5. I see a mobile home on the side of the hill,
Surrounded by what looks like daffodils:
Some that survived the wintry chill,
I see.

6. I see an eighteen wheeler turned up on its side;
They said fire broke out and the driver died;
Ambulance took him for his last ride,
I see.

7. I look at the sky, nothing to see;
I want to know and I want to believe.
I feel the heart beat inside of me, and,
I see.

Before I record an album of my songs, I take a songwriting trip. That is, I actually go somewhere on a trip and think about nothing except songwriting and songs in general. I was on such a journey when I wrote "I See." I drove my own car, traveled alone, and did not have a planned route in mind. I simply got into my car, took a handheld tape recorder, camera, note pad, and a guitar, and took off across the country. My working album title was "Natural Dreams." I drove to where interstates 65, 40, and 24 intersect in Nashville. I did not make up my mind to head north until I reached that intersection. For some unexplainable reason, I headed toward Lexington, Kentucky. It was February, and the roads were all pretty bad; but the best radio weather report seemed to favor I-65. So that could have been the reason I decided to head north. After spending the night in a little roadside motel in Lexington, I got an early start northward the next morning at nine o'clock.

Talking into the handheld tape recorder gave me a good recollection of what I had seen on my trip. Sometimes I would actually hum a little melody or sing a few lines into the recorder. Two days later I found myself at a motel in Lewisburg, West Virginia. I was sitting on the side of the bed playing back the notes I had made on the recorder. While making these notes I had thought each of the things I had seen on my trip could be an idea for a song. After I had played the tape a few times and taken notes on the legal pad, it started to dawn on me that there was a pattern to the observations I had made.

I am not in the habit of talking to myself; but on this occasion I leaned back on the bed and said, almost aloud, "I see." That, of course, jarred my writing mentality and gave me the title for the song. It was then that I started to put meter and rhyme to the song, and, without more ado, that's how it was written.

I have taken many such trips during my writing career. One of my best albums is titled "In Search of a Song."

I should mention that a person can have a lot of misadventures out on the road alone, without a planned route and daydreaming about songwriting in the process. However, I find this singularity of purpose a healthy thing for my own writing and recommend it to other writers, although I advise you neither to turn down too many dead end roads nor check into any motels that don't give you an inside latch on the door. It's strange to get a phone call in your room at two in the morning when you're the only person in the world who knows who and where you are.

I hitchhiked to Chicago and back one winter with one change of clothes in an old duffel bag, just for the experience of being out there on the road with folks different from me. I wouldn't recommend that kind of trip to anyone because there are definitely some "other kinds" out there on the highways of America.

Songwriting can get to be a dangerous business if you love it the way I do.

"I Flew Over Our House Last Night"

I love to tell the story of how I wrote "I Flew Over Our House Last Night." As with many songs, it began as a joke. Connie Smith, one of country music's great entertainers and singers, and I were flying in a private plane from Warren, Ohio, to Nashville to do a cerebral palsy telethon. On the way, we flew over my hometown in eastern Kentucky. I told Connie at the time, "I'm going to write a song called 'I Flew Over Our House Last Night.'"

We were amused by the phrase *I flew over*. The statement *I flew over our house last night* conjures up images of a person in a Superman uniform leaping tall buildings in a single bound. With a line of this kind you are suggesting a humorous premise, which is supported by a serious lyric. Having heard the song after what initially appeared to be a comical opening line or title, people have said, as if to their utter amazement, "Hmmm! That's really good!" This shows you can use the element of surprise to good advantage.

Naturally, it is very difficult to describe a melody to someone who hasn't heard it. As best I can, I will tell you why I used this particular melody. The mood was suggested by the soft flowing of the airplane through a beautiful, starlit night. As described in the song, the moon was full and shone brightly in a cloudless sky. The city was visible below. Having established in my mind the basic mood of the melody, I constructed the song around it. My mental processes ran approximately as follows: Picture a successful businessman-type in a jetliner, perhaps separated for some reason from a girl he had loved or a woman he had been married to. Now they are living in completely different worlds. On this particular evening, he is flying over her house.

In my mental picture, the sweetheart is in her night clothes, asleep, with her hair tousled about her head. The moon is shining, and she is sleeping peacefully while the man in the airplane is traveling to another destination, perhaps on some business venture.

Thus we have two people who are close to one another and yet so far away—both mentally and physically. He is only 30,000 feet above her; but she doesn't know he is there, creating a rather melancholy, romantic mood.

I FLEW OVER OUR HOUSE LAST NIGHT

By TOM T. HALL

2. For just one second I thought I was back in town;
The man your friends all say has only brought you down.
The airline hostess asked me, "Sir, are you sure that you're all right?"
I FLEW OVER OUR HOUSE LAST NIGHT.

2nd. CHORUS: Thirty thousand feet below me, you were fast asleep,
And thirty thousand feet above above, I almost stopped to weep.
I wonder did you toss and turn as I roared out of sight;
I FLEW OVER OUR HOUSE LAST NIGHT.

Hallnote Music

P. O. Box 40209 - - - Nashville, Tennessee

To write the song, we actually sit with the man inside the plane and look at everything from his point of view because he is conscious of the situation. The woman is not; she is asleep. So we have his narrative. This song is, of necessity, his monologue; it is his stream of consciousness that brings the song into play, describes the evening, his emotions, and what has happened in the past. As he passes over the house, the stewardess asks him why he is so melancholy. He obviously has a sad expression and perhaps a tear in his eye. At the end of the song we see the plane "roar out of sight," bringing an automatic conclusion as he goes on to other things.

Before starting on the lyrics, or doing any other work on the song, we have created a situation. We will know exactly what we are going to write about before we begin. I think this is very important. I have found this method works best for me. Let's find all of our characters and put them in the proper perspective. What sort of day or evening is it? Where is everyone? What character and personalities do they have? What are their motivations and reasons for making any sort of comment at all on the situation?

"I Flew Over Our House Last Night" is a melancholy little story of love that didn't work out, revealed to us through the comments of a man sitting in his airplane seat and reflecting on the woman, their relationship past and present, and the locale. We just play it out with our melody.

MORE ABOUT JOHN HENRY

By TOM T. HALL

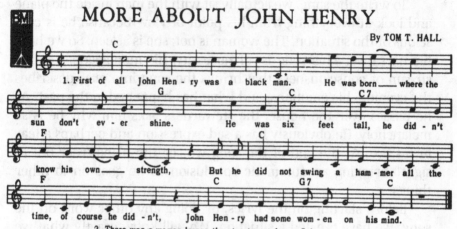

1. First of all John Henry was a black man. He was born____ where the
sun don't ev-er shine. He was six feet tall, he did-n't
know his own____ strength, But he did not swing a ham-mer all the
time, of course he did-n't, John Hen-ry had some wom-en on his mind.

2. There was a woman 'cross the street named poor Selma,
Loved John Henry like a natural man.
John Henry quit poor Selma just like he was quittin' work,
He loved that stinger-ree of Julie Anne's, and what is it?
A stinger-ree is something else you understand.

3. There was a man named Stacker Lee in Argenta,
A little man with a big forty-four;
You know he shot his woman down and took a shot at poor Selma,
But ole Stacker won't be shootin' anymore, he had to quit it,
John Henry laid him dead on the floor.

4. John Henry threw Stacker Lee in the river,
Then he said I've got a say so to say;
He broke out in a song that was wrote by Blind Lemon,
Said Julie Anne, I'm singing my say. He said I love you,
But I do not like your low down ways.

5. Well, John Henry went to a conjuring woman,
Said this misery ain't no way to live.
Somebody's back door creepin' on my pretty Julie Anne,
Conjure woman had a say so to give, she said, John Henry,
She said that's just the way things is.

6. Well, John Henry went to a hell busting man,
Said I'm tormented deep in my soul.
That hell buster prayed John Henry's sins away,
And they tell me that the thunder did roll,
Sweet Jesus, what a frightening sight to behold.

7. From that day on John Henry was a changed man,
All he did was just work all the time.
He worked till the muscles in his body gave out,
Then he kept right on a-working in his mind;
Don't do it, 'cause a man ain't s'posed to work all the time.

8. Julie Anne said John Henry I love you.
Poor Selma said John Henry, you're my man.
Ruby said, I'm gonna cook you up some greens and some lean meat
With cornbread in a four foot pan, with lots a cracklins,
But John Henry was a different kind of man.

9. Well they allow that hard work killed John Henry;
I'm gonna leave that allowin' up to you.
Well, was he killed by hard work or was he killed by bad women,
Be sure that this ain't happening to you;
Quit working when your day's work is through. *(Ad lib - fade)*

"More about John Henry"

This is a song I think you should study closely. In it I have used a public domain melody. This means that the melody, in this case quite well known, has outlived the limitation of copyright and belongs to anyone who cares to use it. I have used a brief spoken introduction to give some background and explain the reason for the song.

I found an old book that told me the true story of John Henry. From it I learned that John Henry, contrary to the legend surrounding him, had several girlfriends. Among them were Poor Selma, Julie Anne, and Ruby. John Henry's life was as complicated by his romances as by the many jobs he had. He was not only a steel driver, but also a cotton rouster, among other things. In the town of "Argenta" he was pretty much of a playboy, who had been involved with narcotics, had been in fist fights, and had suffered a considerable amount of emotional turmoil.

In using the P.D. melody to the old "Legend of John Henry," written many years ago and handed down through generations, I felt I had half the song already written because I didn't need to be concerned with the melody.

In the lyrics, I pointed out that John Henry didn't swing a hammer all the time, but that he also frequently had some women on his mind. I also pointed out that John Henry lived in a time when he met several other interesting characters. For instance, I was surprised to learn that John Henry knew a man named Stacker Lee, who was probably the character found in other folk legends named Stagger Lee, about whom a popular rhythm and blues song is based.

By using these old P.D. melodies and variations on the folk themes, I could tell interesting new stories, translate the hero and other people in the song into modern-day characters, and make it all relevant to our time. With this in mind, I mention in the song that "a man ain't supposed to work all the time" and that John Henry was probably killed as much by his involvement with bad women as by his hard work. We can see that people now are working too hard and running too fast, just as John Henry did then. We hear of corporate executives having heart attacks, ulcers, and growing old before they should. Many of them are quitting their jobs and returning to the more casual lifestyles of the country, rather than trying to maintain the hectic urban and suburban pace.

In analyzing this song, you will see that a number of the reasons for a song's success a hundred years ago are equally valid today. As I have maintained throughout this book, in songwriting we are dealing with universal thoughts—love, fear, hate, and anxiety. Many of our own emotional problems and almost all of our basic human emotions are universal. People are concerned about them today just as they were generations ago.

I think the lesson to be learned from the song "More About John Henry" is that it is possible to take an old folk song, a P.D. melody, and a poem by an unknown author and make these into songs acceptable to the present generation because they deal with the basic emotions of people.

"Old Dogs, Children, and Watermelon Wine"

Being the author of "Old Dogs, Children, and Watermelon Wine," I find it difficult to see all the things in the song that have made it successful. A man cannot know all there is to know about himself. But I will tell you why I wrote the song the way I did, and perhaps in reading the lyrics you can discover more about the song and more about me than I have learned myself.

I opened the song with a question, "'How old do you think I am?' he said." First, try to get the attention of the listener. The public will listen to you, but, just like a mule, you must first get its attention. Thus the unusual opening line.

In writing the song, I attempted to do two things. I tried to get sympathy for the narrator (by placing him in a bar in Miami sipping blended whiskey) and for the old man (by having him be an old man). I established his advanced age by mentioning he is past sixty-five. In my estimation, just being an old man gives him license to be a philosopher.

We have established the location; the old man is working in a bar in Miami, talking to a fellow sitting there. The subject of the song is the old man's philosophy, which is that there are only three things in the world worth a solitary dime: old dogs, children, and watermelon wine.

Seldom will I write a song without mentioning a woman somewhere in it. The reason is that I have been told that women buy 80 percent of the records sold in this country. True or not, I rarely leave them out of my songs. In this song, I added a line that is part of the old man's philosophy, that "women think about theyselves when menfolk ain't around." Now you may not believe this, but I tried to say a little something about women's liberation. I tried to imply that women have things to do and think of besides men. Some women were rather put out by the line. They said, "What do you have against women? You said in your song that they think about themselves when men aren't around." I countered by saying, "It is not my philosophy; it is the old man's. That's what he said, and I am only quoting him in the song." Thereby I narrowly escaped a lengthy dissertation on what women do when menfolk aren't around.

Old Dogs, Children, and Watermelon Wine

By TOM T. HALL

(Spoken) How old do you think I am? He said. I said, well I didn't know. He said, I turned sixty-five about eleven months ago. I was sittin' in Mi-am-i,___ pour-in' blend-ed whis-key down___ When this old grey, black gen-tle-man was clean-in' up the lounge. 2. There was-n't an-y-one a-round 'cept this old man___ and me. The guy___ who ran the bar was watch-in' "Iron-sides" on T.V. Un-in-vit-ed he sat down and o-pened___ up his mind. On old___ dogs and chil-dren and wa-ter-mel-on wine. wine.

3. Ever had a drink of watermelon wine? He asked.
He told me all about it though I didn't answer back.
Ain't but three things in this world that's worth a solitary dime,
But old dogs, children and watermelon wine.

4. He said women think about theyselves when menfolk ain't around,
And friends are hard to find when they discover that you down.
He said I tried it all when I was young and in my natural prime;
Now it's old dogs, children and watermelon wine.

5. Old dogs care about you even when you make mistakes.
God bless little children while they're still too young to hate.
When he moved away, I found my pen and copied down that line
'Bout old dogs and children and watermelon wine.

6. I had to catch a plane up to Atlanta that next day,
As I left for my room I saw him pickin' up my change.
That night I dreamed in peaceful sleep of shady summertime
Of old dogs and children and watermelon wine.

In the line "I saw him picking up my change," I credited the old man with humility. He was apparently retired, and this was perhaps a part-time job cleaning the tables in the little bar. I felt this gave his philosophy even more credibility; it stated he would take a tip for the service he performed and he was not above making a few extra dollars through honest labor.

As the narrator, I involved myself personally with the old man's philosophy by dreaming that I, too, was enjoying the old dogs, the children, the watermelon wine, and the shady summertime.

When writing a song, remember that every line is important. You have only a short time in which to get your message across to the people. Given the opportunity of an entire line in which to say something, do not just make it rhyme with the line before it, but make it meaningful, sincere, lending credence to the message of the song. This gives the tone of the song a continuity and makes it more believable. I have often mentioned incidents that seemed of little importance to the overall thought of the song; yet, upon hearing these comments and observations, people are moved to agree, "Yes! Of course! That's just the way it was."

Personal viewpoints and observations can add credibility to your song.

RAVISHING RUBY

By TOM T. HALL

RAV-ISH-ING RU-BY, ___ ___ she's been a-round for a-while;
RU-BY, ___ ___ be-lieve an-y-thing ___ you say,

RAV-ISH-ING RU-BY, ___ ___ she was a truck-stop child, ___
Just like her dad-dy said, he said he'd be back some day; ___

Born in the back of a rig some-where ___ near L. A., ___ RAV-ISH-ING
She ___ was just ___ four-teen, she grew up wild and free, ___ And all the

RU-BY, ___ you've poured a lot of hot ___ cof-fee ___ in your day. RAV-ISH-ING
time she's been wait-ing on ___ him, ___ she's been wait-ing on

2. you and me. RAV-ISH-ING RU-BY, she sleeps in a bunk out back,

Her days and nights are filled with dreams of a man named Smil-ing Jack. ___

That was her dad-dy's name, and that's all she ev-er knew; ___

RAV-ISH-ING RU-BY, ain't got time ___ for guys like me and you.

3. RAVISHING RUBY, beautiful young girl now;
RAVISHING RUBY, she made a solemn vow.
Waiting on Smiling Jack, he'll come rolling by.
She wants to see him, she wants to touch him
either way dead or alive. *(Repeat Chorus)*

Hallnote Music

P. O. Box 40209 · · · Nashville, Tennessee
MADE IN U.S.A.

"Ravishing Ruby"

I'm going to tell you about "Ravishing Ruby," how I came to write the song, and where I got the idea. As a friend and I drove through Redding, California, one morning, we stopped at a truck stop for breakfast. When we walked in, one of the truck drivers recognized me, jumped up and waved, and inquired as to the nature of my health and the intent of my journey. He wanted to know about my songs and music. We discussed songwriting, entertaining, and where I get my ideas. Then he asked me to sign an autograph for a girl he knew at one of the truck stops on the West Coast. Her name was Ravishing Ruby.

On the way back to the bus after breakfast, I reflected on that discussion about songwriting and the source of my ideas. It dawned on me that I probably had just picked up another idea for a song. "Ravishing Ruby." Of course!

On the bus in which my band, *The Storytellers*, and I travel, I always have a guitar. I took it from the case and started strumming and singing the line "Ravishing Ruby." Then I got to thinking about what sort of person she could be. In my mind I could see her as a tall, dark, lovely young woman with long black hair, beautiful eyes, and a sensitive mouth. I took her to be a sincere and quiet person.

After forming this mental picture of Ravishing Ruby, I tried to determine where she had come from. I took the liberty of creating an origin, a lifestyle, and a purpose in life for her. I pictured a girl, abandoned by her father in a truck stop when she was fourteen, growing up and working there while waiting for her father to return. I saw her father as a slim, cowboy-type truck driver who laughed and smiled a lot and was carefree and happy. I gave him the name Smilin' Jack.

Then I wondered what sort of living conditions Ruby would have at this truck stop, having lived her life there from age fourteen until the present time, having grown up into a beautiful young lady. I pictured the customary bunk out back, since in truck stops around the country there are places for the truck drivers to shower, shave, and rest. This generally consists of a bunk that is rented out. So, I thought Ruby would have a small place in back of the truck stop, with one of these bunks and probably some pictures of Tom Jones, Elvis, and Merle Haggard on the wall. I created an entire existence for Ruby, her disposition, her purpose for staying at the truck stop all those years, what she looked like, some of her motivations.

Again, we have completed our cast of characters, their personalities and background before we proceed with work on our lyrics or melody. In a very simple process, I put all the information into the song. In the lyrics, I indicated she was waiting for her father to return and was more interested in this than in all the truck drivers who came by to flirt with her, date her, or become familiar with her.

The melody of the song, for those who don't read music or who have not heard the song, has a Spanish or south-of-the-border lilt to it, suggestive of the mariachi music of the southwestern part of the United States. We included marimbas and Spanish horns in the production of my record to further the Spanish mood. I decided on this type of melody because of the West Coast location and the strong Spanish influence in this area, with the suggestion that Ruby could be Spanish, or part Spanish.

I kept this in mind while defining Ruby's character as well. Rather than take a person with the name Ravishing Ruby who lived on the West Coast and make her nationality French, or to use a type of music more native to the East, I kept the whole thing West Coast-oriented and kept my thinking centralized.

In writing any song, I recommend that you use this process. Once you have determined what you want to write about, be sure to keep in mind that in your music you are creating a situation that is real, believable. Perhaps knowing the process I used for this song will help you remember to be as logical in your thinking as possible. For instance, there would be little need to make Ravishing Ruby a midget unless it served some purpose. There would be little need to make her a boisterous person, since her main purpose in life is waiting for her father to return. And, again, there would be little need to use any music not associated with the nationality of the character.

If you hear an interesting name or meet an unusual person, remember not to be too incredible in being creative. The song will become uncomfortable for the listener, and your characters will be unnatural and difficult to define.

DON'T FORGET THE COFFEE BILLY JOE

By TOM T. HALL

1. It snowed the night be-fore and it had fall-en on the ground. We did-n't have a car and we lived sev-en miles from town, And I can hear my dad-dy's voice so man-y years a-go, say-ing, DON'T FOR-GET THE COF-FEE BIL-LY JOE.

CHORUS

Ma-ma needs her med-i-cine, she's got that real bad cough; We'll get our check on Mon-day, tell old Sam we'll pay him off, And you can catch a ride when you get to the black-top road, DON'T FOR-GET THE COF-FEE BIL-LY JOE.

2. Me and Quinton went back on the hill and we cut some wood;
Burning in that old warm morning stove, it sure smelled good.
Daddy couldn't get work then and I was just a child,
And God was on vacation for a while.

CHORUS: Well, if you see Fred, you tell him I'll come help him kill them hogs,
And ask him if he'd still be interested in my dog.
Don't hang around that pool room all day, we might get more snow,
And DON'T FORGET THE COFFEE BILLY JOE.

3. Well, they wonder why there ain't no rabbits left this day and time;
To tell the truth I guess we ate 'em all in forty-nine.
Was that yesterday or was it over twenty years ago,
DON'T FORGET THE COFFEE BILLY JOE. *(Repeat 1st Chorus)*

"Don't Forget the Coffee, Billy Joe"

I have chosen this song to make a point about relating true situations. I have a brother named Billy Joe, so the song, although philosophical at times, is basically true.

Among my favorite subjects are things that have really happened to me, places I have been and people I have met. I have, in fact, made a career of this sort of writing. I find it very simple to write this kind of song, because instead of creating a situation, as I had to do with "Ravishing Ruby" and "I Flew Over Our House Last Night," I don't have to manufacture attitudes, emotions, and motivations. I know the "what" and "where" and perhaps the "why" of my story because of personal involvement. I assume I know the motivations of the other characters.

In writing a song of this sort, I simply sit down and tell the story as it happened, as though talking with a friend in a coffee shop or in our kitchen. As people will in conversation, I "color" the stories in order to make a point and make observations about things that may have seemed insignificant at the time. "Don't Forget the Coffee, Billy Joe" is a song I enjoyed writing because it saved me a lot of work.

If you have an interesting story from your childhood, of something that happened a week ago, or about an incident that happened to someone else, you have the advantage of prior knowledge of the characters and situation.

Regarding melody, let's go back to that mysterious "something" that makes a melody what it is. In this song, I used a bouncy melody suited to the humorous lines in the song, as well as the bits of irony, pathos, and melancholy. In writing a song incorporating several characters, each with different outlooks on the situation—perhaps one melancholy, one serious, one very practical person—a medium must be struck between the extremes so that all the lines will lie within the framework of the melody as comfortably as possible.

If the whole subject of the song is melancholy, the melody should be slow to suit this mood. If the song is to be boisterous in subject matter, perhaps about a brawl or the gunfight at the OK

Corral or a shootout at Blackrock, the melody should be something up-tempo to carry the action through the song. The music can then enable the singer to dramatically express the action and fury surrounding the situation.

This would be a very good practice for you. Begin by writing songs for which you already have the situation in hand, with a mental picture of what happened, of the emotions and attitudes of people. I think you'll find it a fascinating way to entertain your friends. As your friends, they are interested in what you have done and what you are doing, and it is rewarding to put one of your own experiences into a song, rather than just sitting and talking about it.

How I Wrote "I Love"

"I Love" is one of the simplest songs I have written, from the standpoint of plot structure. It's obvious I have used a formula, the "rhyme each line" and "rhyme within a line" method. Example:

> I LOVE little baby ducks
> Old pick up trucks
> Slow moving trains . . . and rain

The first two lines rhyme, and then I rhyme within the line with *trains* and *rain*.

Once I have established this pattern, it also gives me a chance to perk up the ears of the listener by dropping the rhyme within line method and using a different sound at the end of some verses. Example: tomatoes on the vine . . . and onions.

Vine and *onions* do not rhyme; however, I feel that the first two lines rhyme strongly enough to hold the song together while I make a little point that some of the things I love are not of a rhyming nature.

I really enjoyed writing this song. I immediately knew I had a universal thought when it dawned on me that no one had written a song called "I Love." Oh yes, there had been songs about loving Paris, Alice, trains, and all sorts of people and places, but there had not been one that simply said, "I Love."

I was sitting at a desk at my publisher's making some phone calls when I got the idea. It had been a beautiful fall morning, and I was in a good mood, as I love any of the changes of the seasons. I suppose the one reason the song has so many references to spring is that it seemed so far away at the time.

Just about every office in Nashville has a guitar, so I picked up the one that was nearby and began to strum the melody as I wrote down the list of things I really love and appreciate.

The line about "grass" really threw me for a minute; almost as soon as I had written it I knew that someone would think the grass in my song was a reference to marijuana. I personally think that grass is about 20 percent of the beauty of nature; it is the carpet on which a lot of the furniture of flowers and animals is spread. Once

I LOVE

By TOM T. HALL

1. I LOVE lit-tle ba-by ducks, old____ pick-up trucks,
Slow mov-in' trains and rain. I LOVE lit-tle coun-try streams, sleep with-out dreams,
Sun-day School in May and hay, And I LOVE you, too.

2. I LOVE leaves in the wind, pictures of my friends,
Birds in the world and squirrels.
I LOVE coffee in a cup, little fuzzy pups;
Bourbon in a glass and grass,
And I LOVE you, too.

3. I LOVE honest open smiles, kisses from a child,
Tomatoes on a vine and onions.
I LOVE winners when they cry, losers when they try,
Music when it's good and life and I LOVE you, too.

© COPYRIGHT 1973 BY

HALLNOTE MUSIC
P. O. Box 40209 · · · · Nashville, Tennessee 37204

I had made up my mind to go ahead and use the word *grass*, it was no longer a problem to me. I knew the word meant what I wanted it to mean, and nothing more. Or should we say, nothing less.

More Song Lyrics

Now you're on your own. Here's a small cross-section of some more of my songs. I know you have no idea of the initial inspiration, but you can analyze them. Take a look at the rhyming patterns, the meter, the devices used to get and hold attention, lyric development, and continuity.

I just wish I could be on hand while you dissect these songs. You might very well uncover some songwriting principles that I am only doing unconsciously.

A WEEK IN A COUNTRY JAIL

Words and Music by TOM T. HALL

2. They said tomorrow morning
   You can see the judge, then go,
   They let me call one person on the phone.
   I thought I'd be there overnight
   So, I just called my boss
   To tell him I'd be off, but not for long.

3. They motioned me inside a cell
   With seven other guys,
   One little barred-up window in the rear.
   My cellmates said if they had let me
   Bring some money in,
   We ought to send the jailer for some beer.

4. Well, I had to pay him double
   Cause he was the man in charge,
   And the jailer's job was not the best in town.
   Later on his wife brought
   Hot bologna, eggs and gravy;
   The first day I was there I turned it down.

5. Next morning they just let us sleep
   But I was up real early,
   Wonderin' when I'd get my release.
   Later on, we got more
   Hot bologna, eggs and gravy, and,
   By now I wasn't quite so hard to please.

6. Two days later when I thought
   That I had been forgotten
   The sheriff came in chewin' on a straw.
   He said where is the guy
   Who thinks that this is Indianapolis?
   I'd like to talk to him about the law.

7. I told him who I was
   And told him I was working steady
   And I really should be gettin' on my way.
   That part about me being
   Who I was did not impress him;
   He said, "The judge'll be here any day."

8. The jailer had a wife
   And let me tell you she was awful
   But she brought that hot bologna every day.
   And after seven days,
   She got to lookin' so much better
   I asked her if she'd like to run away.

9. Next morning that old judge
   Took every nickel that I had
   And he said, "Son, let that teach you not to race."
   The jailer's wife was smiling from the
   Window as I left;
   In thirty minutes, I was out of state.

HARPER VALLEY P.T.A.

Words and Music by TOM T. HALL

1. I want to tell you all a sto - ry 'bout a Har - per Val - ley wid - ow'd wife

Who had a teen - age __ daugh - ter who at - tend - ed Har-per Val - ley Jun - ior High.

Well, her daugh - ter came home one af - ter - noon and did-n't e - ven stop to

play. She said, "Mom, I got __ a note here from the

Har - per Val - ley P. T. A." __ (Spoken) The note said, __ .

(Recitative)

2. The note said, Mrs. Johnson, you're wearing your dresses way too high—
It's reported you've been drinking and a-runnin' 'round with men and going wild.
We don't believe you ought to be a-bringing up your little girl this way—
It was signed by the secretary, Harper Valley P.T.A.

3. Well, it happened that the P.T.A. was gonna meet that very afternoon—
They were sure surprised when Mrs. Johnson wore her mini-skirt into the room.
As she walked up to the blackboard, I still recall the words she had to say.
She said, "I'd like to address this meeting of the Harper Valley P.T.A.

4. Well, there's Bobby Taylor sittin' there and seven times he's asked me for a date.
Mrs. Taylor sure seems to use a lot of ice whenever he's away.
And Mr. Baker, can you tell us why your secretary had to leave this town?
And shouldn't widow Jones be told to keep her window shades all pulled completely down?

5. Well, Mr. Harper couldn't be here 'cause he stayed too long at Kelly's bar again.
And if you smell Shirley Thompson's breath, you'll find she's had a little nip of gin.
Then you have the nerve to tell me you think that as a mother I'm not fit.
Well, this is just a little Peyton Place and you're all Harper Valley hypocrites."
No, I wouldn't put you on, because it really did, it happened just this way,
The day my mama socked it to the Harper Valley P.T.A.

THE YEAR
THAT CLAYTON DELANEY DIED

By TOM T. HALL

Moderately fast

(TAG: Last time) (Well) I re - mem - ber the year ___ that Clay - ton De - lan - ey
Clay - ton was the best ___ gui - tar ___ pick - er in our

died; They said ___ for the last two ___ weeks ___ that he suf - fered and
town; I thought he was a he - ro and I used to fol - low Clay - ton a-

cried. It made a big im - press - ion on ___ me, ___ al-
round. I of - ten won - dered why Clay - ton, ___ who

though I was a bare - foot kid. They said he got re - lig - ion at the
seemed so good to me, Nev - er took his gui - tar and

end ___ and I'm glad that he did. ___
made it down in Ten - nes - see. ___

3. Daddy said he drank a lot, but I could never understand;
I knew he used to pick up in Ohio with a five-piece band;
Clayton used to tell me, "Son, you better put that ole guitar away,
There ain't no money in it; it'll lead you to an early grave."

4. I guess if I'd admit it, Clayton taught me how to drink booze;
I can see him half-stoned, pickin' out "The Lovesick Blues."
When Clayton died, I made him a promise I was gonna carry on somehow;
I'd give a hundred dollars if he could only see me now.

5. I remember the year that Clayton Delaney died.
Nobody ever knew it, but I went out in the woods and I cried;
Well, I know there's a lot of big preachers that know a lot more than I do,
But it could be that the Good Lord likes a little pickin', too. *(to Tag at beginning)*

BACK POCKET MONEY

By TOM T. HALL

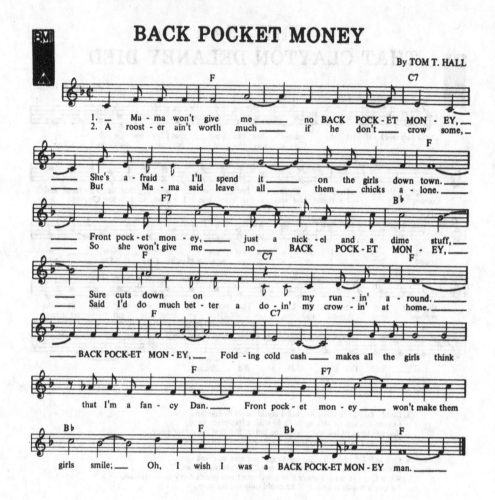

D.J. FOR A DAY

By TOM T. HALL

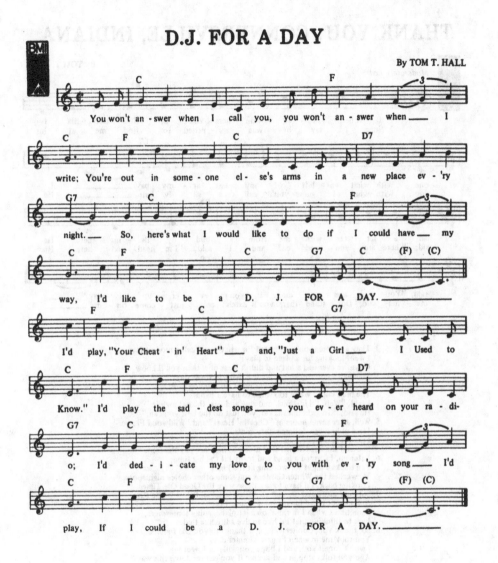

THANK YOU, CONNERSVILLE, INDIANA

By TOM T. HALL

1. I rolled in - to Con - ners - ville in Nine - teen Six - ty-
2. Need I say he was sur - prised to find me at his

one, With what was left of my last ar - my pay. _____ I
door, With what I guess you'd call a sil - ly grin. _____ He

had a let - ter with me from a bud - dy liv - ing there. He
said, "Where are you head - ed?" and I said, "I'm head - ed here." His

said, "You stop and see me if you're ev - er up this way." _____
ma - ma said, "Don't stand there, you'll catch cold, just come on in." _____

3. They gave me room and board for what you'd call a modest fee;
   I went looking for a place to play;
   If you've ever had a hat and didn't wear one, then you'll know
   The way a country singer made a living in those days.
4. The menu printed on the window of the bar and grill;
   The man said, "We're too small to have a band."
   I said, "Well, I'll just pick and sing and pass the hat awhile."
   He said, "Go right ahead, kid, you just do the best you can."
5. Well, after seven hours of "Cheatin' Heart" and "Wildwood Flower"
   I had only seven dollars eighty cents.
   I gave it to a waitress who was gonna have a baby;
   She said she needed just that much to help her pay the rent.
6. Later on, I formed a band and really hit the big time;
   Ten bucks a night for working at the Pines.
   We worked the Winter Gardens and some other choice nightspots.
   Looking back, I'd have to say those were the Good Ole Times.
7. Summer came and me and ole Mitch Mitchell fished White River,
   And caught those big ole juicy channel cats;
   Sometimes when I'm ridin' on a jet plane, going somewhere,
   I get to thinking that I'd like to live a life like that.
8. So, thank you, Connersville, and thanks to you Ole Indiana;
   You took me in when I knew slimmer days.
   I won't forget you, and I hope you will not forget me,
   And you folks stop in and see me if you're ever down this way.

THE POOL SHARK

By TOM T. HALL

3. Little Red Parker was away in the back, taking quarters and handling racks,
   I told him, "Red, come up here and glue 'em up tight."
   That brandy had me feeling warm; I tipped that waitress and checked her form;
   I said, "Honey, you look like a winner," and she just smiled.
4. I played like a man with a broken wrist. I won two and he won six.
   I had him set up, so I said, "Let's play for five."
   By this time a crowd had gathered round to see this fish and watch him drown.
   I told that waitress, "More brandy, water by."
5. He went out and got a custom cue; he said, "It's no offense to you,
   But I don't play off the wall with nobody but friends."
   It had gold initials and a leather grip, pearl and silver inlaid tip;
   He smiled at me and said, "Why don't we play for ten?"
6. Well, I've never seen a man that walked, who made those balls and table talk;
   They were speaking English and he sure didn't need my help.
   He broke the balls and kept that string for a hundred eighty-seven bucks and a ring,
   Till I gave up and said, "Friend, you'll have to play by yourself."
7. Well, he sucked it up and he walked outside; I strolled out just to watch him ride;
   There was a blonde in a Caddie, built like the rest of that car;
   The boys in the pool room had 'em a laugh; I hung it up and I let it pass;
   Didn't have a thing, but elbows to put on the bar.
8. The waitress smiled, and said, "Water by"; I took the charity and thanked her twice.
   Sitting there sipping, when suddenly, I had me a thought;
   Unlucky gambler, lucky in love, I guess you know what I was thinking of,
   When I said, "Waitress, honey, what time you get off?"

I WASHED
MY FACE IN THE MORNING DEW

By TOM T. HALL

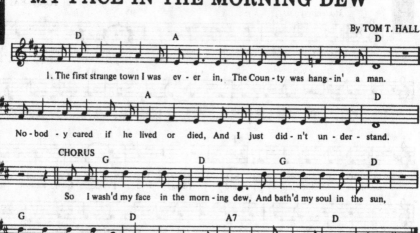

1. The first strange town I was ev-er in, The Coun-ty was hang-in' a man.

No-bod-y cared if he lived or died, And I just did-n't un-der-stand.

CHORUS

So I wash'd my face in the morn-ing dew, And bath'd my soul in the sun,

Wash'd my face in the morn-ing dew And kept on mov-ing a-long.

2. The second strange town that I was in,
   They were laughing at a poor crippled man,
   Begging for nickels and dimes on the street,
   And I just don't understand.

3. The third strange town that I was in
   Was settled peaceful and nice.
   The rich got richer and the poor got poorer,
   And to me it didn't seem right.

4. Someday times are bound to change,
   It can't be very far,
   And each injustice I have seen
   Will come before the bar.

ME AND JESUS

Words & music by TOM T. HALL

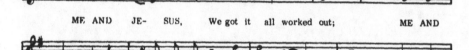

Chorus

ME AND JE- SUS, We got our own thing go- ing,

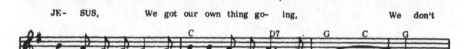

ME AND JE- SUS, We got it all worked out; ME AND

JE- SUS, We got our own thing go- ing, We don't

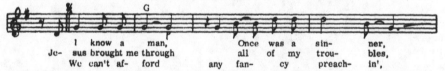

need an- y- bod- y to tell us what it's all a- bout.

I know a man, Once was a sin- ner,
Je- sus brought me through all of my trou- bles,
We can't af- ford any fan- cy preach- in',

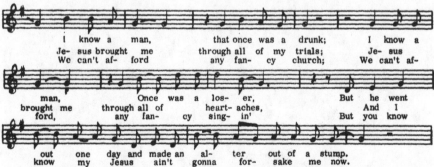

i know a man, that once was a drunk; I know a
Je- sus brought me through all of my trials; Je- sus
We can't af- ford any fan- cy church; We can't af-

man, Once was a los- er, But he went
brought me through all of heart- aches, And I
ford, any fan- cy sing- in' But you know

out one day and made an al- ter out of a stump.
know my Jesus ain't a gonna for- sake me now.
Jesus got a lot of poor people out a 'doin his work.

CHAPTER 20

What Some Great Songwriters Say

Johnny Cash:
Member of Nashville Songwriters Association International Hall of Fame, elected 1977. Writer of "I Walk the Line" and "Folsom Prison Blues."
"Write with simplicity. Simplicity is complicated."

Jerry Chestnut:
Writer of "Four in the Morning" and "A Good Year for the Roses."
"All songwriters write songs, but a successful songwriter relates life and love by marrying words to music in such a way that people who hear it associate with it and like it enough to go out and buy it."

Dallas Frazier:
Member of Nashville Songwriters Association International Hall of Fame, elected 1976. Writer of "Elvira" and "There Goes My Everything."
"A professional songwriter does not have to be controlled by temperamental moods. He is like a carpenter; he can build, whether he feels like it or not. We must decide to write."

Harlan Howard:
Member of Nashville Songwriters Association International Hall of Fame, elected 1973. Writer of "Busted" and "Heartaches by the Numbers."
"Fred Rose said, 'Hit songs are written, standards are re-written.' I wish I had said that."

Bob McDill:

Writer of "Amanda" and "Baby's Got Her Blue Jeans On."
"From the first to the last word nothing should be wasted. Every line should point to the center or title line."

Curly Putnam:

Member of Nashville Songwriters Association International Hall of Fame, elected 1976. Writer of "Green, Green Grass of Home" and "He Stopped Loving Her Today."
"I believe that simplicity is the key to writing hit songs but with enough depth and feeling to touch people in all walks of life. Love and loneliness always work for me."

Sonny Throckmorton:

Writer of "Middle Aged Crazy" and "Last Cheaters Waltz."
"The way you write songs is to do a lot of writing; practice makes perfect. Love what you do."

Cindy Walker:

Member of Nashville Songwriters Association International Hall of Fame, elected 1970. Writer of "You Don't Know Me" and "Take Me in Your Arms and Hold Me."
"Songs are a commodity just like milk, bread and meat. People have to have their songs. It's up to the songwriter to see that their songs are nourishing, good food for their spirits."

A Parting Shot

At the risk of repeating myself, I would like to sum up my philosophy on songwriting. Throughout this book I have tried to keep a tone of cautious optimism. No project, hobby, or job (especially a labor of love), should be taken up with doubt or dread. Songwriting should be fun. It should be inspiring, but it also should be fun.

If we start out wondering if one song or another will be a big hit, we are defeating our purpose. Let things happen as they will. The song must come first. All other events surrounding the future of that song are, and will always be, in the hands of many others. Only the public knows whether it likes a song; and one person liking it will not make it a commercial success. I have found that the happy-go-lucky people are the most successful. Ralph Emery, host of numerous television and radio shows, has a saying we should all remember. He calls it the Eleventh Commandment: "Do Not Take Thyself Too Seriously."

I have always marveled at an entertainer pouring out his heart in a sad song of lost love or other misfortune on stage while the audience yells and screams its approval. What is it in entertainment that causes people to cheer and applaud wildly at the misfortune of others? It is a small mystery of our culture and civilization. I am telling you that the saddest song will bring joy to the hearts of your listeners because people want to be entertained.

Songwriting is a great hobby. Not every writer will enjoy commercial success and not every writer will live to see his or her song become the rage. Some compositions have laid dormant for years until someone came along who needed such a song. When Abraham Lincoln scribbled his Gettysburg Address on a piece of paper while riding a train, he had no idea that one day it would be celebrated as one of the great speeches of all time. In fact, he said, "The world will little note, nor long remember what we say here!"

I have often lamented that some of my favorite songs are tucked away inside albums that are out of print. I sometimes wish they could have been single records and given the chance to star in the galaxy of good songs. I wrote them anyway, knowing their destiny, yet feeling that the effort was worthwhile. They're still my songs, and one day they might spiral out of the groove and into the heart or mind of a listener somewhere.

In the preface of this book I mention that I wrote my first song as a sort of practical joke. That's a darned good attitude, if we are not to be washed away by our own egos and unrealistic ambitions.

This book has been a labor of love for me. I have intended it for the thousands of people that I meet on the byways of life who have an interest in this most unusual of hobbies and occupations. I hope it has brought you an understanding of the craft.

Have some fun, and always remember, "If it don't fit, don't force it."

Discography

Ballad of Forty Dollars, Mercury

One Hundred Children, Mercury

Homecoming, Mercury

In Search of a Song, Mercury

I Wrote a Song About It, Mercury

I Witness Life, Mercury

We All Got Together And . . ., Mercury

The Storyteller, Mercury

For the People in the Last Hard Town, Mercury

Country Is, Mercury

The Rhymer and Other Five and Dimers, Mercury

Songs of Fox Hollow, Mercury

Faster Horses, Mercury

About Love, Mercury

Magnificent Music Machine, Mercury

New Train, Same Rider, RCA

Saturday Morning Songs, RCA

Ol' T's in Town, RCA

Tom T. Hall Greatest Hits, Mercury

Tom T. Hall Greatest Hits, Vol. II, Mercury

Tom T. Hall Greatest Hits, Vol. III, Mercury

Places I've Done Time, RCA

Live at the Opry, RCA

Soldier of Fortune, RCA

The Storyteller and the Banjo Man, CBS

Everything from Jesus to Jack Daniels, Mercury

Natural Dreams, Mercury

Song in a Seashell, Mercury

Index

Printed in the USA
CPSIA information can be obtained
at www.ICGtesting.com
LVHW051533210724
785408LV00008B/109